Living in God's Time

Living in God's Time

A Parent's Guide
to Nurturing Children throughout
the Christian Year

Margaret McMillan Persky

UPPER
ROOM BOOKS ™
NASHVILLE

Scripture quotations not otherwise identified are from the New Revised Standard Version of the Bible, © 1989 by the Division of Christian Education of the National Council of the Churches of Christ in the USA. Used by permission.

Excerpt "Litany" in chapter 7 from *Litanies for All Occasions* by Garth House. Used by permission of Judson Press.

Excerpt in chapter 7 from *The Revised Common Lectionary*. Copyright © 1992 The Consultation on Common Texts (CCT), P.O. Box 840, Room 381, Nashville, TN 37202 USA. All rights reserved. Reprinted with permission.

Cover Design: David Uttley Design
Cover Photograph: Digital Stock
First Printing: 1999

The Upper Room® Website http:/ / www.upperroom.org

The Library of Congress Cataloging-in-Publication Data
Persky, Margaret M., 1942-
    Living in God's time : a parent's guide to nurturing children throughout the Christian year / by Margaret M. Persky.
        p.   cm.
    Subtitle on cover: Parent's guide to nurturing children throughout the Christian year.
    ISBN 0-8358-0875-0
    1. Christian education—Home training. 2. Church year—Study and teaching.
I. Title. II. Title: Parent's guide to nurturing children throughout the Christian year.
BV1590.P425   1999
248.8'45—dc 21   98-55212

Printed in the United States of America

To my parents,

MARY MAUDE AND NORRIS MCMILLAN,

who nurtured me in the faith

and showed me what it means

to live a life in relationship to God.

To my son,

DR. NEAL E. PERSKY,

who once with childlike wonder

and now with a rare adult honesty

believes in me, yet challenges me

to be more than I think I can be.

CONTENTS

Preface   9

Introduction   13

1. The Shaping Experience   19

2. Shaped by a Crossroads: Advent   27

3. Shaped by God's Gift: Christmas Season   43

4. Shaped by a Different Way Home: 55
Epiphany of the Lord and Season after the Epiphany (Ordinary Time I)

5. Shaped by the Distance from the Head to the Heart: Lent   67

6. Shaped by Water (Resurrection): Easter Season   81

7. Shaped by Fire: Day of Pentecost and Ordinary Time II   91

8. Shaped by a Child: Kingdomtide (Ordinary Time III)   107

Epilogue: Living in God's Time Check   117

Small-group Guidance   121

Appendix: A Calendar of the Christian Year   138

Notes   140

"I saw Jesus!" an excited four-year-old shouted in response to the guided meditation I had just completed with her Sunday school class. I sat down in the circle to listen as all the other four-year-olds joined in: "I saw Jesus, too." Thus began my formal entrance into the world of young children and their spiritual development.

In the years following, as I hungrily searched to understand more about the spiritual life of children, I read the works of Maria Harris, Robert Coles, Jerome Berryman, and Patricia W. Van Ness. Children do indeed have a rich spiritual life, but they need adult guidance in giving language to that life. Through experiential and formational methods of teaching, adults can provide an environment of openness within children that gives room for the Holy Spirit's working in their lives. We can help them name what they have experienced, acting as cofashioners with the Creator in the shaping of God's children.

More exciting than all of my reading were my experiences with the children themselves. Guided meditations, prayer rituals inviting children to pray aloud or silently, "I wonder" sessions (in which I moved the children to contemplate different aspects of the biblical story they had heard by saying "I wonder why . . ."), and one-on-one conversations as I listened to them tell me about their pictures of God: these all convinced me that children live in a spiritual world while we adults spend much time trying to reclaim the spiritual world we had as children. Author Michael Yaconelli says in his book *Dangerous Wonder*, "When we [adults] reclaim our child-likeness, we stumble upon the presence of God—and we are amazed to find the place all children know about: the place where we once again hear the whisper of Jesus."

When JoAnn Miller of the Upper Room® called and said to me, "We want you to write a book for us. Tell me where you find passion in your work," I immediately responded, "Faith development and how it happens intentionally and unintentionally in the home." I knew immediately that my own family faith experience would be the shaping focus of this book. Since my own child was grown, it was important to me to be able to discuss and field test my ideas with those actively engaged in the shaping of children in their homes. I also felt it was important to gather the wisdom of members of the congregation, other Christian educators, and grandparents. So I invited members of my church to become part of a small family known around the church as "Margaret's Lab Group." Some family members were young with small children at home, some had teenagers at home, others were married with no children, others were divorced with children, still others were grandparents now living alone, and some were single. All had experiences growing in faith as well as helping children to grow in faith. The group represented faith traditions of United Methodism and other Protestant denominations, Catholicism, and Judaism.

At each meeting we reflected on the previous liturgical season and how we had experienced this season at home. We then looked at the present season and discussed how families could intentionally live, shape, and experience this season in their homes.

Reflecting on my own childhood stories, helping others to reflect on their childhood stories, and discussing how faith took shape intentionally or unintentionally in our childhood as well as how it presently happens in our homes, I realized anew how powerfully family influences faith development. Without question, those with whom we live, play, and work shape our lives as we shape theirs. I am more convinced than ever that our attention as parents to that shaping invites a lifelong relationship between God and our children.

I am eternally grateful to JoAnn Miller, Executive Director of Book Publishing at Upper Room Books®, for the courage she displayed in asking me, a novice, to author a book. With wisdom, insight, and gentleness, she encouraged me every step down the unknown trail.

Thanks to editor Holly Halverson, who gave structure and clarity to my many, many pages.

Words can never express my appreciation to the Reverend Gina Gilland Campbell for the countless hours, the endless red ink, the scissors and tape she used as she performed surgery on my manuscript. I thank her for her gifts of time and critique, but most of all, I thank her for her friendship.

I wish to express my appreciation to those members of Laurel Heights United Methodist Church who joined together in "Margaret's Lab Group" as family to consider how we mold the people around us. Thanks to Janis Arnold, Aleene Block, Alison and Taylor Boone, Janice Collins, Thad Dorsey, Jerrie Jackson, Barbara Nardi Kurtz, Ann and Mike McGlone, Heather and Richard Miller, and Connie Hooper and John Shaffer.

I thank those countless pastors, Christian educators, extended family, and friends who continue to form me as one of God's children. But most of all, I give thanks to the God who shapes me as the potter shapes the clay.

The leader picked up the clay and began molding it in her hands. As she shaped it she said, "The great Lord God picked up the dirt and began molding it as a potter molds clay. God shaped the dirt in God's likeness. Then the great Lord God breathed life into it. And God said, 'It is good.' Throughout the generations God continues to shape, and to reshape, that which God made.

"God is the potter and we are the clay. As God shapes us, so we shape the people and the space around us. Sometimes we do this intentionally and faithfully. And sometimes we do this without any conscious awareness at all."

The leader referred to the two kinds of faith shaping that take place: intentional and unintentional. *Intentional faith shaping* occurs when we make conscious decisions to act, believing that these decisions will form others and us in the image of God. These decisions are about religious activities, how we treat friends, how we spend money, how we discipline, or any other issue of life.

Unintentional faith shaping happens as our children watch us relating to others, resolving conflict, and managing money. It occurs when we do not make conscious decisions about shaping, or even take time to evaluate how actions and events shape others around us or ourselves.

As I study the accounts in Genesis 1 and 2, God's creation seems to reflect the intentionality and unintentionality of our own human creations. Scripture states clearly that God intentionally created the world and all that is in it and said, "It is good." God intentionally shaped us in God's own likeness, giving us the creative responsibility of caring for the earth. And God intentionally gave people the freedom of choice, but this freedom itself gives an unintentionality to God's creation because people often choose to create without putting God first.

Reflecting on my life, I see both intentional and unintentional faith shaping. My mother and father intended that as a family we would go to church every Sunday. We lived in a small ranching community in the hill country of Texas with extended family living all around us. Because we were ranchers and the land and stock needed our care, because family was present to us, and because vacations were not needed as stress relievers, we stayed at home on the weekends. Sunday school and worship attendance provided the focus for our family's weekends.

As a child, I knew it was inappropriate to ask the question, "Do I have to go to Sunday school and church today?" But when I was a high school youth burdened by a heavy homework load, one weekend I said to my parents, "I have homework to do. Can I stay home from youth group?"

"No," came the response, "you should have planned to do your work earlier in the weekend." The Sunday agenda was nonnegotiable. And it was a gift. Every week I experienced the peace of a tradition that allowed time for resting in God through the worship and study of God, the enjoyment of extended family, and the beauty of God's creation.

Unintentional shaping often took place on Sunday afternoons as we participated in extended family gatherings, eating lunch around the table while sharing stories of the family and of the community. William H. Willimon, author of *Sunday Dinner: The Lord's Supper and the Christian Life*, states that at his grandmother's dinner table he learned what it meant to be a Willimon and how Willimons lived. I believe that at my grandmothers' tables I learned the same thing. I learned who I am and, more importantly, whose I am. First,

I understood, I belonged to God, and then to the family created by my mother and father.

If I wanted the family's approval, I listened to their stories to see which persons had their approval and which persons did not. If I wanted to know more about God I asked, or better yet, listened as my mother and her three sisters (representing two Protestant denominations and Roman Catholicism) debated theologically the issues of the day and the role of the church.

At an early age my cousin Carl and I dramatized these discussions. My grandmother's treadle sewing machine became our church altar. Carl would recreate the setting for catechism class as he experienced it and I would recreate the setting for Sunday school as I experienced it. When we disagreed on the setting of the altar, the liturgy, or the teachings of the church, we raced to consult with our mothers, who naturally supported us in the understanding of our own church.

Therefore at an early age I learned not all persons who believed in God believed or acted in the same way. I learned to listen to varying theological positions and to decide what I believed. Early in my faith journey, "doing theology" (discussing how I relate to God, how I relate to others, and how others relate to God) naturally shaped the clay of my spiritual being.

Carl's mother and my mother did not agree upon an educational method for teaching Carl and me about the faith. They just did it—unintentional shaping passed from one generation to the next.

Some Sunday afternoons we napped at home. Then my parents and I climbed into the pickup truck to drive across the ranch. My dad's identity as a rancher provided unintentional shaping in my life. Though my father never talked to me directly about God, I learned much about God from him. As we drove across the pastures and my dad discussed the rain, the growth of grass, the price of cattle and goats, I came to understand he believed the land to be a gift of God. He understood himself to be the steward of that gift. He believed he bore the responsibility of the care of the land. He took care not to overgraze or overstock, and to produce the best livestock he could without abusing the land.

I learned at a young age how the ranching business and my family depended on God. A rancher has no control over the weather. The rains come and the rains go. Freezing weather that kills livestock sweeps down unannounced. Market prices drop while feed prices rise excessively. A rancher can do his best and still have no control over his family's income. During the six-year drought of the fifties you could smell the few remaining blades of grass burning in the hot July sun, and my father would say, "It will rain again. We just have to hold out until it does." Shaped by the drought and the other uncontrollable elements of ranching, the true essence of dependence and waiting in hope in God formed parts of my spiritual clay.

In this book I invite parents and caregivers of children and youth to consider how faith shaping takes place in their lives by sharing stories of faith shaping from my own life and the lives of others. I invite you to see yourselves as you really are: potters who shape clay, your children. As you read these stories, I hope you will remember your own history and begin to understand how you took shape as a child of God. Look at how all those everyday acts in your family of origin spiritually shaped the clay of the lives comprising your family today.

This book follows the liturgical seasons of the church year because these seasons give form and shape to God's time, *kairos* time. The story of Jesus Christ as revealed through the liturgical seasons helps shape us as disciples of the Christian faith. I encourage you as a family to use the liturgical seasons to give shape and form to God's time in your individual and family life.

Each liturgical chapter ends with a section called Living in God's Time. Here you will find a Weekly Family Worship Ritual and Activities meant to help you parent more intentionally. Each chapter closes with a guide for Family Reflection on the Season. The work of Jerome Berryman, Episcopal priest, teacher, and author of *Godly Play*, greatly influenced these sections. "Godly play," a method of Christian education and spiritual direction for children, draws them inward, helping the children to be more fully aware of the mystery of God's presence in their lives. For example, children are encouraged to enter into Bible stories and relate them to their personal experiences. I have known preschoolers, teens, and adults who have experienced this method on a regular basis and noted the depth of their spiritual maturity and understanding.

In Living in God's Time, I also suggest intentional ways of addressing developmental issues for children and youth that arise with a high level of predictability. Author Carole E. Calladine suggests in her book *One Terrific Year* that seasons and significant events in a child's year directly affect the child's behavior. For example, the beginning of school often causes children and youth to seek an identity for the new setting. As parents, with some preparation we can respond in intentional ways to these predictable events.

And that is the whole point: preparation, as an act of intentionality, gives direction to your desire to see your child shaped into a young person and adult aware of living in God's presence. Use your enthusiasm carefully. As you approach the ideas in this book, don't try to do everything! Choose one or two ideas or suggestions in each season. See what works and what doesn't in your home. Adjust these ideas to suit your family. Reflection questions at the end of the chapter can help you evaluate how you have lived the season in your home, choose which parts you wish to keep, and decide what you might change for the same season next year.

I strongly suggest that parents and churches form small groups to read and discuss each chapter. I have included a guide for these groups. Preferably, groups should read the chapter on Advent and have the group meeting several weeks before Advent begins. Families then have the opportunity to prepare and work together.

All of the stories, suggestions, and activities are given to help you, the parent as potter, to more meaningfully shape your children, your clay. As God fashions us so we fashion the people, particularly our families, around us. May we do so with the same care and intentionality as God uses with us.

The Shaping Experience

The cotton T-shirt is a staple of U.S. dress. Almost everyone has a stockpile of favorites. We wear them for different reasons, though. Some of us wear oversized T-shirts to hide our shape. Some of us wear smaller-sized T-shirts to flaunt our shape. Some of us want T-shirts to fit just right, not too tight and not too loose. When we wear a T-shirt, we reveal much of our outer shape.

A T-shirt reveals something of the inner shape of a person, too. We wear T-shirts naming groups with whom we associate. We announce to the world our likes and dislikes through the logos and slogans that appear on our T-shirts. Our own special brand of humor comes through in the T-shirts we choose. Those who design their own shirts reveal truths about themselves through their creativity. Buttons from a grandmother's button box decorate a T-shirt sharing family heritage with the world. Bluebonnets on T-shirts announce that we're from Texas or have recently visited the Bluebonnet State. Sometimes we unintentionally share something of ourselves when we carelessly toss on a T-shirt without considering the message. Other times we spend hours looking for just the right T-shirt to purchase for ourselves or someone else. For some, T-shirts top their collectible list.

We spend much of our time and money attempting to change our outer shape. We buy into diets and health programs supposedly endorsed by the medical community, "blessed" by God, or tested by celebrities. We purchase shape-changing devices through mail-order companies. We have become health fanatics and worship at the altar of health and exterior appearance instead of at the altar of God.

Carlyle Marney, Baptist minister and theologian (1916-1978), stated in a sermon he called "The Nerve to Submit":

> We have made images of the self and believed our images enough to worship them. We have wrapped ourselves in layers of feathers—we have worshipped views of ourselves and our surroundings—we have our views of our race, our religion, our economics, our sex, our class, our nation—all our treasures![1]

While I believe God calls us to be good stewards of our health and outer bodies, God does not call us to make our exteriors the primary focus of our lives. God evaluates us by something else entirely.

WHERE THE LORD LOOKS

The Bible tells us that God sent Samuel to choose a new king. When Samuel met Jesse and seven of his sons, he felt certain that the king he sought stood before him. The Lord encouraged Samuel to look with care, "for the LORD does not see as mortals see; they look on the outward appearance, but the LORD looks on the heart" (1 Sam. 16:7). And one by one, the Lord rejected the seven eldest, good-looking sons of Jesse. Then Samuel asked Jesse to send to the pastures for his youngest son. The Lord told Samuel to anoint the youngest of Jesse's sons, not because of his equally handsome outer appearance, but because of the unique shape of his inner being.

God cares about the shape of our hearts. God sent Jesus that we might see the shape of true personhood. When we choose to follow Jesus we open our hearts to be shaped in the image of God. And as we are shaped, we too shape those in our influence. As I mentioned in the Introduction, there are two kinds of shaping that take place, intentional and unintentional. Here are some thought-provoking examples of each.

We intentionally encourage youth to become members of the church community yet often unintentionally negate the validity of their membership. Usually we fail to include them, though they are full members of the worshiping community, in the decision making about the major programs at the church. During a church stewardship campaign I heard one junior high youth remark, "They don't ever ask us to give stewardship talks. They only ask the adults!" The stewardship committee had not intentionally chosen to exclude youth as stewardship speakers, but this young woman felt excluded.

Unintentionally, the congregation shaped her life. How will she respond? When she becomes an adult, will she exclude youth, too? Or will she remember her experience and as an adult use the experience as a reminder from God that youth participate in congregations as full members of the body of Christ? As our spiritual clay has been shaped, so we shape the spiritual clay of others.

A junior high youth group intentionally planned an evening of fellowship at a nearby bowling alley. A junior higher stepping onto a chair suddenly faced a bruiser of a man who announced himself as the owner. The group received orders to leave immediately. No warnings! No discussion! No negotiation! An intentionally planned evening of fellowship was seemingly ruined.

Back at the church the group debriefed. How could the group have acted differently so as to reflect the light of Christ? How could the group respond at this moment to reflect the light of Christ? Letters sent to parents informed them of this unfortunate incident. Youth signed a letter of apology to the owner of the bowling alley. Leaders believed this to be the best learning experience of the year. Unintentional shaping flowed from an intentional plan!

No one will ever know with certainty how persons come to be shaped in the likeness of God. We may never know if our intentional decisions to shape in the image of God do so. Mystery surrounds the process of the human heart and life growing increasingly in God's likeness. But we as parents can make decisions toward this most important shaping. We can parent intentionally, doing our best and trusting God to complete the work.

SHAPING THROUGH STORY

We do know with certainty that for centuries, the people of God have believed in the power of intentional shaping through story. In Deuteronomy 6 we read Moses' commandments:

> Hear, O Israel: The LORD is our God, the LORD alone. You shall love the LORD your God with all your heart, and with all your soul, and with all your might. Keep these words that I am commanding you today in your heart. Recite them to your children and talk about them when you are at home and when you are away, when you lie down and when you rise. Bind them as a sign on your hand, fix them as an emblem on your forehead, and write them on the doorposts of your house and on your gates. (Deuteronomy 6:4-9)

Moses commanded the Israelites, and us as God's people, to pass on the biblical stories that tell of the relationship between God and God's people. These stories reveal to us who we are and whose we are. They shape us intentionally in at least three ways. First, they describe the development of the relationship between God and God's people. They reveal how we became the people of God. Second, the stories serve as a mirror. We see in them how a faithful person lives. We have a standard to which we can compare our daily living. And third, they tell God's people how to fashion the pattern of their daily lives—how to live in awareness of and response to God's presence.[2]

We open ourselves to be shaped by biblical stories, in the beginning, by reading them. We read them as individuals, as families, and with the people of God. Then we begin to look for ourselves and our own experiences in the Bible stories. For example, if we have been afraid, do we identify with Peter walking on, and sinking under, the waves (Matt. 14:22-33)? If we have searched for healing, do we identify with the woman who touched the hem of Jesus' robe (Matt. 9:20-22)? If we have been overwhelmed on a beautiful morning, do we share the joy of the author of Psalm 19? In time, as we study the stories in the Bible, we grow skillful in identifying the connections between the happenings of our lives and the lessons of God.

We then face the challenge not just to be able to tell the story, but to see ourselves as a story God would tell. Just as God worked through the circumstances, events, and relationships in the lives of biblical people long ago, so God works in the same way in our lives today. As we learn to make these connections between biblical story and personal story, we give ourselves over to be intentionally shaped in the image of God.

Family stories shared from one generation to the next shape us just as our personal stories do. As with individual stories, family stories about circumstances, happenings, and relationships can connect with the story of God.

Stories of immigrant families from faraway places moving to new lands of promise may be similar to the story of the journey of the Hebrew people as they left Egypt and headed to the Promised Land (Exod. 3). Stories of a child dreaming of a time he won't feel left out may touch the story of Joseph, cast out into slavery by his jealous brothers but eventually reconciled to them (Gen. 37-45). Stories of a man who lost everything—health, family, possessions—but came then to understand God's eternal presence in his life may be like the story of Job.

MAKING CONNECTIONS AS A FAMILY

You can practice making biblical connections to contemporary life as a family. First, celebrate the gift of story in your family. Read and tell biblical, personal, and family stories to one another. Develop the spiritual discipline of looking intentionally for God in your life as individuals and as families. Work at making the connections. Look to identify God at work in all the stories.

Second, offer your children the gift of silence. Each day, perhaps before bedtime, help them to experience a short period of quiet reflection. Encourage them to look for God in the daily events, circumstances, and people in their lives. This habit will benefit them all their lives.

Third, as a family share the gift of the liturgical or church year. Use the seasons to look at *who* and *whose* you are as you retell the story of the life, death, and resurrection of Jesus Christ.

Fourth, create a family worship center. It should be a place that family members often see and where they can comfortably gather. It might be the center of the family dining table, the mantle over the fireplace in a family room, or a small table centrally located in the family living area. Make it appealing, a place where family members will like to be. Agree to treat this area as "holy space." And develop a family covenant addressing how family members will treat one another any time they gather at their worship center. This covenant should contain no more than three or four conditions for faithful family living. For example:

Family members will listen to one another.
Family members will honor what others say as valid for the speaker.
Family members will look for the good in each other.
Family members will all have an opportunity to share.

And finally, give at least as much attention to improving your interior shape as you do your exterior. Yes, it's more difficult than changing T-shirts, but it's also more important. Open your heart to God's shaping. Be attentive to how you have been shaped. Increase your awareness of the ways you shape others. Give thanks that God's shaping continues throughout your life journey.

Shaped by a Crossroads: Advent

At this time of year, we stand at the crossroads of time. One road sign reads, "*Chronos* Time." We all know people who walk this road. They are driven by the passing of minutes and hours, days and weeks. They constantly check watches, time clocks, and calendars. Their lists and agendas rule the day. They eschew birthday parties, moan at each New Year, and sigh over the alarm clock every night. Complaints mark their conversation: *Too few hours in the day! Too few weeks in the year! I should have accomplished more by now!* These people are always in motion; they are brisk, breathless—and discontented. To them, the invisible is merely that. All that matters is today's tangible crossed-off to-do list and adding fresh items to tomorrow's.

The other road sign reads, "*Kairos* Time." We know a few of these folks, too. Those who choose this road don't charge—they walk, with confidence. They too heed the clock and calendar, but only as points of reference. They see time not as an enemy but as a companion; as they walk along with it, life changes, but life—and change—is good. Lifelong goals inform their schedules, but a goal missed today might be made up tomorrow. All things have their appointed time, so rest is available, peace is possible, and joy is always at hand. Those on the *kairos* road live within a calm assurance that all things work together for the good of those who love God; within a calm awareness that in the midst of the frantic demands of everyday life, God is at work doing a good work in them, through them, even in spite of them. They are more relaxed than those harried by *chronos* deadlines and can open themselves more readily to God's leading. All that really matters is using today to see and reflect the Creator; tomorrow will take care of itself.

About sixteen years ago, I stood at such a crossroads. Sitting across the breakfast table from my dad one July fourth morning, *chronos* and *kairos* collided as my dad asked if I would continue with my unhealthy marriage. Suddenly months of hesitation at time's crossroads came to an end. I had to choose. "No," I replied. With that one word the ticking of the kitchen clock ceased and time stood still as my life entered *kairos*.

I found myself looking at the future uneasily. How would I incorporate an awareness of and submission to God in the midst of such a big change? I continued to follow the routine of the *chronos* time clock: managing home and family, fulfilling my responsibilities at work, taking care of daily dilemmas. But in choosing *kairos*, I also entered an experience of God's advent. Advent means waiting—waiting for the birth of God's promise. Waiting to see what God's love will do. Waiting to learn what it means to do and be God's will. Living in *kairos*—holding tenaciously to my awareness of God's presence and care and my desire for God's leading—meant that daily chores became far less important than discovering God's way for me through this crisis. Finding God's will, following God's lead, leaning on God's promises and assurances consumed me. My decision to divorce precipitated my decision to be more intentional than ever in listening to God's guidance. My father's intentional question had pushed me to acknowledge the emptiness in my life—to stop living solely in *chronos* and to participate in *kairos* as well.

During my season of advent waiting, God and I began to wrestle. It reminded me of Jacob's struggle with God (Gen. 32:22-32). I faced the hole deep within my own heart, and the anger living there: anger at a dream destroyed, at God who allowed the destruction of dreams, and at myself for not being wiser. No simple answers presented themselves. I felt little comfort in that hole deep within my heart, yet I knew God's presence.

Struggling, waiting, listening, and walking along the road of *kairos*, new life began to form. My family shaping stood me in good stead during this crisis in my life. It had taught me to find God in all of life: the God who worked in our lives as we ranched the land, the God whose love surrounded us in our grief, the mystery of God when there seemed to be no answers, as well as the God who could withstand our questions, our doubts, and our anger. I began to understand that whatever I decided, right or wrong, good or bad, God would be with me. Like Jacob, I would walk away from this wrestling match with a limp. Like Jacob, I would travel *Kairos* Time with God. Like Jacob, I would experience God's grace.

AN ADVENT DECISION

Like this advent season of my life, our church Advent season places us at the crossroads of time. New Year's represents *chronos*, the beginning of the physical year. Advent represents *kairos*, the beginning of the church's liturgical year. As we enter this season of waiting and preparation for the birth of God's son, we retell God's story through the life of Jesus, the Christ. The circular Advent wreath reminds us that God's time makes a circle. When we mindfully make *kairos* part of our thinking, we realize that God's love encircles our very being in both its emptiness and its fullness. In *kairos* all beginning points become ending points and all ending points become beginning points, each laden with God-given possibilities. We begin to live in awareness of the hope God offers.

During Advent, the church asks pivotal, intentional questions of us. Will we choose to honor God's presence in an attitude of *kairos,* and enter into a time of waiting and preparing to receive once again the mystery of Christmas? Will we spend more time at home with the people we love? Will we choose a slower pace, different rituals to help us wait and prepare for the coming of Christ? Will we draw inward, listening for God's will for our lives? Will we look for God among the details of the day and discover the ways Christ is reborn in us?

Or will we choose *Chronos* Time and race through the four weeks preceding Christmas? Will we push and shove our way through the malls? Will we speed through red lights and dodge bumper-to-bumper traffic? And as December 25 draws closer, will we be swept up in a frenzy of gift buying, baking, decorating, partying, and attending special church and school activities, while we still try to maintain our routine of work and home? Will *chronos* or *kairos* be the shaping force for us this Advent? Will intentional or unintentional shaping take us through this season of waiting? Will our relationship with God be a part or the center of our preparations?

Choosing *Kairos* Time becomes a problem for modern-day persons. It rubs against our impatient nature. Waiting nine months to know the sex of our offspring proves difficult, so we have a sonogram to tell us the sex of our baby. Garden nursery parking lots become a danger zone in the spring as people rush to purchase plants so that yards burst into full bloom overnight.

Call waiting interrupts our present telephone conversation to signify some-one else wants to talk to us. Our culture strives to make waiting obsolete.

Scripture reminds us of those who waited upon the Lord: Zechariah and Elizabeth (Luke 1:5-25, 57-66), Mary (Luke 1:26-45), Simeon and Anna (Luke 2:22-38), and the remnant of the people Israel, to name a few. Listen to the words that most often greeted these people: "Do not be afraid. I have something good to say to you." God knew then and knows now that wait-ing can be scary for those who live expecting instant answers. God invites us to wait in hope, trusting in God's mercy.

Waiting for the birth of child . . . to receive a lab report . . . for semester grades . . . to hear the outcome of an interview . . . to see a relationship grow or terminate—these seasons of advent waiting offer us opportunities to turn inward, to deepen our relationships with God and one another, to address pivotal questions. So it is with Advent. If we choose *Kairos* Time, we open ourselves to all the possibilities of God. We allow God's time to shape us.

CHILDREN AND ADVENT

As excitement for Christmas Day builds and fatigue increases, children can become caught in a tug-of-war between the spirituality and the commercial-ity of the season. They too feel the pull between *chronos* and *kairos* thinking. The paradoxes become more glaring. Children bounce between baby Jesus and Santa Claus, giving and getting, wise men and Rudolph, the cold, dark stable and the warm, festively lit hearth. What adults separate with ease can confuse children.

Adding to the confusion, we often model for our children and youth that appropriate actions result in gifts. God didn't say to God's people, "I will give you my son if you are obedient to my will." God gave us Jesus out of graciousness. An attitude founded in *chronos* thinking sees tit-for-tat giving; *kairos* thinking clears the way for the truth: Christmas is about God's love, Jesus' sacrifice.

In busy environments, as children sense the anxiety in their homes, fear may become a looming factor. Children living in single-parent homes may be anxious about where and with whom they will spend Christmas. They may worry over the feelings of the parent left alone. Youth may fear not being included in the right parties, not having dates to the party, or not having clothes appropriate to the special event. When we parents take the slower and more deliberate walk down *Kairos* Time, we invite our children to speak with us in deep ways and allow them to voice their fears, as together we address them. We draw them to look for God's presence and help in each difficult situation. We lead them to pray.

Sometimes the children lead us. By December 24 a preschooler had chosen *Kairos* Time over *Chronos* Time. When asked, "Why are you so excited?" he replied, "Tonight we get to put baby Jesus in the manger."

HOW WILL WE WAIT?

The season of Advent awaits us. We must choose how we will watch and wait for the coming of the Christ child. How will we prepare our hearts and our homes to receive the gift of Christ once again into our lives? How will we let Christ be the focus for our lives throughout the year?

My lab group worked at intentionally choosing *kairos*. Together we explored these questions: How can we slow down during the season of Advent? How can we help the family to experience this time of waiting? How can we make time to allow God to work in our lives?

When we met in January, to my surprise and delight one by one they shared changes they had made from previous Advent seasons. One family was remodeling their home and intentionally decided not to get out all the Christmas decorations. They put up a tree with simple ornaments, gathered around their Advent wreath once a week, and the father consistently avoided the shopping malls. A second family decided to try less "fuss and bother": no lights on the outside of the house, fewer decorations inside. A third group member went to the shopping mall only once and in a record time of forty-five minutes, purchased all his gifts for his wife.

All present that evening agreed they had chosen to spend more time on the *kairos* road. Simpler and fewer decorations and less time in malls filled with frantic people gave birth to more family time. Some of the parents used the time to explain to their children that the focus during Advent should be the coming of Christ, not the house with the most decorations. Other families used the time to wait upon the birth of Christ through family Advent rituals. They had all made beginnings that were endings and endings that were beginnings. All would repeat their practices next year, adding a time of reflection around one family meal a day.

God beckons us to choose *Kairos* Time. Families who do strengthen their relationships to God and one another. They step more deeply and meaningfully into the mystery of Christmas. They embrace more fully the literal incarnation of the past, and the ongoing presence of the Christ in the present.

LIVING IN GOD'S TIME:

WALKING IN *KAIROS* TIME DURING ADVENT

Preparing the Home Worship Area

Prepare the family worship space for Advent. A table covering or underlay of a "royal" color, such as blue or purple, might be the base of the worship area. For this season you will need an Advent wreath with candles. Families can make their own wreath or purchase one; some families prefer to "save the trees" and use an artificial wreath. Have handy also a small candle-snuffer to extinguish the candles, and figures representing the Holy Family (Mary, Joseph, baby Jesus, prophet, shepherds, kings, donkey, and sheep).

The Advent wreath appears on the first Sunday of Advent in our churches and our homes, signifying our arrival at the Crossroads of Time. A family member could make a signpost which reads "*Kairos* Time" and "*Chronos* Time." *Kairos* Time might point to the Advent wreath while *Chronos* Time points to a calendar or to a door leading outside.

In the home, place the wreath in the worship center on the blue or purple underlay. Mark this event with Blessing the Advent Wreath (see Ritual that follows).

Add the figures representing all the characters of the story of Jesus' birth to the worship center week by week. This enhances the time of waiting and the liturgy of the Advent wreath. If possible, use figures made of olive wood or some other quality, nonbreakable substance that allows children of all ages to touch and play with the figures while you tell the story. The beauty of these figures reminds us of the beauty of God's gift.

Invite discussion during the time the family gathers around the Advent wreath. "I wonder" questions enhance spiritual formation by opening the door for all kinds of answers; they allow the questions to touch the child or adult where he or she is at that particular moment. They also often help start conversation:

- I wonder why the angel said to Mary, "Do not be afraid."
- I wonder why God thought Mary would be afraid.
- I wonder what Mary and Joseph thought as they settled in the cold stable that night.

Be sure to allow a few moments of silence after each question to let the children's minds work. Don't feel rushed.

Feel free to reword these questions in age-appropriate language if necessary. Make sure everyone in the family understands that the questions have no right or wrong answers. Any response can be appropriate. This frees them from focusing on correctness and ignites their imagination. Adults and children alike will probe both their minds and their feelings for responses. Don't be alarmed if responses are slow at first. With practice, your discussions will start more readily and deepen.

Draw the conversation from historical discussion to contemporary life. Make it personal. For example, as the children focus on Mary's fears, move them to think about their own fears. Show them how Mary's trust and obedience helped assuage her fears, and how they can practice those same disciplines. As you reveal to your children that God's care for Mary extends to them, *kairos* thinking is at work. Your children begin to apply a biblical precedent to everyday living.

Gather around the wreath at a designated time each week to light the appropriate candles. Use the weekly rituals to highlight the symbolism of the Advent wreath and encourage *kairos* thinking. Prepare each week by prereading the ritual section and assigning members of the family to read, to light and extinguish the candles, and to move the nativity figures. Make sure every member of the family has a responsibility. Together, the rituals and activities will enhance your family's *kairos* preparation for the mystery of Christmas.

Bless the Advent Wreath

Leader: Gather the family around the Advent wreath. Explain the symbolism of the wreath and its candles: *The traditional circular wreath reminds us that God, like the circle, has no beginning and no end. A live evergreen wreath symbolizes our everlasting relationship with God, the source of continuous new life. The wreath's four candles mark the four weeks of Advent waiting. The three purple* (or blue) *candles represent the royalty of Christ. The pink candle represents joy. We place a white candle, the Christ candle, in the center of the wreath, on Christmas Day.*

Reader: Read Matthew 25:1-13.

Leader: Invite discussion about what this parable tells about the season of Advent. Allow for silence before anyone responds to each "I wonder" statement.

 • *I wonder why Jesus called some of the bridesmaids "wise" and others "foolish."*
 • *I wonder how you think the wise bridesmaids felt when the bridegroom came.*
 • *I wonder why Jesus wants us to "keep watch."*

Prayer: *Now, O God, bless this wreath and our family as we prepare to celebrate the mystery of Christmas. May there always be room in our hearts for your son Jesus, the Christ. Amen.*

Family Worship Ritual for the

First Sunday of Advent

Leader: *God's people waited for hundreds and thousands of years for the birth of God's son. We still wait today. We wait and prepare our hearts during the season of Advent to celebrate once again the mystery of Christmas. The prophets help us to wait.*

Reader: Read what the prophet Isaiah said in Isaiah 9:2, 6.

Leader: *To help us wait, we light the prophecy* (first purple) *candle. We place the prophet by his candle to remind us how long God's people waited for the birth of God's son. Let us enjoy the light of the prophecy candle as we think about Isaiah's words.* (Allow for silence before anyone responds to each "I wonder" statement.)

• *I wonder what Isaiah meant when he said that the light would overcome the darkness.*

• *The sun and moon provide sources of exterior light. I wonder what some sources of inner light are.*

• *I wonder what darkness there is in addition to the darkness of night.*

• *I wonder whom the prophets called "the Light."*

As we enjoy the light of the prophets, they will help us wait as we move along the road toward the manger.

Prayer: *O God, sometimes we find it very hard to wait. We want everything right now. Help us to wait. Help us to open our hearts to you during this time of waiting, so that we may be shaped in your likeness by the birth of your son. Amen.*

Leader: As the assigned person extinguishes the candles, say, *We extinguish the light of the prophecy candle, knowing that the light of Jesus lives in our hearts always.*

Weekly Family Worship Ritual for the
Second Sunday of Advent

Leader: *Today we mark the second Sunday of Advent and as God's people we continue to wait. We wait and prepare our hearts during the season of Advent to celebrate once again the mystery of Christmas. The prophets help us to wait. Mary and Joseph help us to wait along the road to the manger. Mary and Joseph waited for nine months for the birth of Jesus, God's own son.*

Reader: Read what the angel says according to the Gospel of Luke 1:26-38 and Matthew 1:18-25.

Leader: *To help us wait, we light the prophecy candle.* (Move the prophet between the second purple candle and the pink candle.) *As we continue to wait we light the Holy Family* (second purple) *candle. We place the Holy Family, Mary and Joseph, by their candle to remind us of the months they waited for the birth of God's son. Mary and Joseph help us to wait and to not be afraid as we wait. Let us enjoy the light of the prophecy candle and the Holy Family candle as we wonder.* (Allow for silence before anyone responds to each "I wonder" statement.)

- *I wonder why the angel said to Mary, "Do not be afraid."*
- *I wonder why the angel said to Joseph, "Do not be afraid."*
- *I wonder if you can think of a time when you were afraid while you were waiting for something.*
- *I wonder how we can overcome our fears.*

As we enjoy the light of the prophets and the light of the Holy Family, they will help us wait as we move along the road toward the manger.

Prayer: *O God, sometimes we find ourselves waiting with fear in our hearts. Sometimes we find that fear makes the waiting even more difficult. Open our ears to hear the words of the angel, "Do not be afraid." Help us to wait unafraid. Amen.*

Leader: As the assigned person extinguishes the candles, say, *We extinguish the light of the prophecy candle and the light of the Holy Family candle, knowing that the light of Jesus lives in our hearts always.*

Weekly Family Worship Ritual for

Third Sunday of Advent

Leader: *Today marks the third Sunday of Advent, and as God's people we continue to wait. We wait and prepare our hearts during the season of Advent to celebrate once again the mystery of Christmas. The prophets help us to wait. Mary and Joseph help us to wait. The shepherds help us to wait. They watched their sheep as they waited.*

Reader: Read what the angel said to the shepherds in the Gospel of Luke 2:8-20.

Leader: *To help us wait, we light the prophecy candle.* (Move the prophet between the pink candle and the third purple candle.) *As we continue to wait, we light the Holy Family candle.* (Move Mary and Joseph just behind the prophet.) *Today we light the shepherd* (pink) *candle. We place the shepherds by their candle to remind us of how they watched their sheep while they waited. Let us enjoy the light of the prophecy candle, the Holy Family candle, and the shepherd candle as we wonder.* (Allow for silence before anyone responds to each "I wonder" statement.)

• *I wonder why the angels told the "good news" of Jesus' birth to the shepherds.*

• *I wonder why the shepherds decided to leave their flock to go and see this new baby.*

• *I wonder in what ways your birth brought great joy to your family.*

• *I wonder why the birth of the baby Jesus brought great joy to so many people.*

As we enjoy the light of the prophets, the Holy Family, and the shepherds, they will help us to wait as we move along the road toward the manger.

Prayer: *O God, we wait for the good news of Jesus' birth. Help us to see the good news of Jesus in all that we do this week. Amen.*

Leader: As the assigned person extinguishes the candles, say, *We extinguish the light of the prophecy candle, the Holy Family candle, and the shepherd candle, knowing that the light of Jesus lives in our hearts always.*

Weekly Family Worship Ritual for

Fourth Sunday of Advent

Leader: *Today marks the fourth Sunday of Advent, and as God's people we continue to wait. We wait and prepare our hearts during the season of Advent to celebrate once again the mystery of Christmas. The prophets help us to wait. Mary and Joseph help us to wait. The shepherds help us to wait. The wise men help us to wait. They studied the stars in the sky as they waited.*

Reader: Read how the star guided the wise men to the baby Jesus according to the Gospel of Matthew 2:1-12.

Leader: *To help us wait, we light the prophecy candle.* (Move the prophet between the third purple candle and the first purple candle.) *As we continue to wait we light the Holy Family candle.* (Move Mary and Joseph just behind the prophets.) *We light the shepherd candle.* (Move the shepherds and their sheep just behind the Holy Family.) *Today we light the wise men* (third purple) *candle. We place the wise men by their candle to remind us of how they studied the stars in the sky as they waited for the birth of the baby Jesus. Let us enjoy the light of the prophecy candle, the Holy Family candle, the shepherd candle, and the wise men candle as we wonder.* (Allow for silence before anyone responds to each "I wonder" statement.)

- *I wonder why the wise men studied the stars in the sky.*
- *I wonder what other names we use for the wise men.*
- *I wonder why the wise men didn't follow Herod's instructions.*

The light of the prophets, the Holy Family, the shepherds, and the wise men will help us wait as we move along the road to the manger.

Prayer: *O God, as we wait, help us to listen and look for signs of the birth of Jesus in our own hearts and the hearts of others. Amen.*

Leader: As the assigned person extinguishes the candles, say, *We extinguish the light of the prophecy candle, the Holy Family candle, the shepherd candle, and the candle of the wise men, knowing that the light of Jesus lives in our hearts always.*

Activities

1. Go the library to find a book that tells the story of St. Nicholas, Bishop of Myra, who died in 343 A.D. St. Nicholas gave toys and food anonymously to children. Our Santa Claus represents a distortion of *Sante Klaas,* the old Dutch name for St. Nicholas. Talk about how Santa and gift giving remind us of the greatest gift of all, God's gift of Jesus.

2. As you wait and prepare for the mystery of Christmas in your own home, also reach out to others to help them experience the mystery of Christmas. We move inward, drawing closer to God, in order to move outward, sharing God's love.

• Bake cookies or other goodies and deliver to a neighbor or shut-in.

• Wrap gifts for the needy. Most cities have projects such as Elf Louise, Toys for Tots, etc.

• Buy toys; deliver them to places collecting toys for children in need. Collect secondhand toys. Clean closets and decide what can be shared so that others will have Christmas.

• Make a list of persons from work, school, neighborhood, extended family, and church family who have not experienced the mystery of Christmas or for whom experiencing the mystery of Christmas this year may be difficult due to circumstances. Choose one or two persons from your list and do one of the following: invite them to dinner and the lighting of your family Advent wreath; deliver a plate of cookies to their home; invite them to participate with your family in a special Advent church service; or share a drive to see the lights of Christmas.

Family Reflection on the Season
In mid-January, take time as a family to evaluate your Advent waiting experience. (See suggestions at the end of the next chapter.)

Shaped by God's Gift: Christmas Season

☙

At our worship service on the Sunday following Christmas Day, we celebrated the gift of Jesus by remembering all the gifts of that first Christmas long ago. As the drama of the birth of the infant Jesus unfolded, the characters took their places in the chancel area: Mary and Joseph, baby Jesus, the animals, the shepherds, and the wise men. The donkey carried Mary to Bethlehem. The cow gave her manger and hay. The sheep gave wool for Jesus' blanket. The dove gave her song. And the wise men brought gold, perfumes, and precious oils. In his sermon that morning, the speaker posed this question. "If I, Thad, could go back two thousand years in time, what gift would I have taken to the manger that night?"

After pausing a moment, Thad continued, "I thought long and hard about that. What is the greatest gift I could bring to the baby Jesus? I decided to give him the gift he left with us for eternity before his death some thirty years later— the gift of love. So to you, the Christ child, I bring this baby blanket as a symbol of the love I have for you and the warmth that it might bring to your body."

Thad reached under the pulpit to pull out a pink, blue, and white cro-cheted baby blanket. The blanket did not belong to just any baby. The blanket had belonged to his infant daughter—the very daughter he had given back to God when she died at the age of eight. As one of few in the congregation that morning who knew the story of that blanket, I could hardly swallow as I watched Thad walk over to the crib, pick up the baby Jesus, and wrap him in it.

Thad said, "Oh, how wonderful it would be to pick up the baby Jesus and hold him close to my chest. I would cuddle him and sing to him songs like 'Amazing Grace' and 'Too-Ra-Loo-Ra-Loo-Ra.' Yes, I would even burp him, even though in *The Best Christmas Pageant Ever* Alice Wendleken said, 'I don't think it's very nice to burp the baby Jesus.'"

Thad then read Matthew 22:35-39:

One of [the Pharisees], a lawyer, asked [Jesus] a question to test him. "Teacher, which commandment in the law is the greatest?" He said to him, "'You shall love the Lord your God with all your heart, and with all your soul, and with all your mind.' This is the greatest and first commandment. And a second is like it: 'You shall love your neighbor as yourself.'"

"So this, sweet baby Jesus, is my gift: a blanket, a symbol of my love for you." With these words, Thad sat down. My mind quickly filled with thoughts of the baby Jesus wrapped in the blanket of Thad's love for his daughter. What a gift! What a paradox! Love so great that it entered the world in the human form of Jesus and as a precious daughter. Love so powerful that it overcame death on the cross as well as enabled a grieving father to offer his daughter's baby blanket as a symbol of his love for Jesus.

The giving of gifts—in honor of the greatest Gift—is a tradition we can practice intentionally in light of *kairos*.

HOW A FAMILY CAN GIVE

Christmas arrives! And once again pivotal questions call us to choose the road we want to travel. Will we be stymied in *chronos* thinking: All these extra events are jamming my calendar. How will I find the time to shop? Do I need to give So-and-so a gift since she gave me one last year?

Or will we turn our minds to *kairos* thinking: To whom can I give this year as a celebration of the Gift? What can I give the baby Jesus? In what new way can I worship God this season?

God's gift of the baby Jesus is an example of sacred giving. But we all know how easily materialism can swallow the holiness of giving. We lose sight of it when we make sure that our children receive every *thing* on their lists and more. One Sunday when I asked an eight-year-old if she had had a good Christmas, she responded, "Yes, I got so much that it won't fit in my closet." When quantity replaces quality in our giving, we've missed the point.

Families can work together to maintain the sacred method of giving. We can shorten our list of materialistic wants. We can work together to receive fewer gifts. Extended families can draw names. Parents and grandparents can agree upon the number of gifts to be given per child or grandchild. Children can be encouraged to limit their wish lists to three or four items.

We can learn to appreciate gifts for more than their monetary value by looking beyond the gift to the giver. Why would the giver choose such a gift for us? Does the gift speak of the relationship we share? We can take care to choose a more meaningful than expensive gift. We can make some gifts or think of thoughtful acts that become gifts. We can give of self instead of material goods.

The events of Christmas resonate with God's gift of God's self to us:

In the beginning was the Word, and the Word was with God, and the Word was God. . . . And the Word became flesh and lived among us, and we have seen his glory, the glory as of a father's only son, full of grace and truth. (John 1:1, 14)

Giving of self calls for thoughtful, deliberate, and intentional preparation. In *You Can Choose Christmas,* author Clyde Reid calls this the content of giving. To give of the self, consider the person to receive the gift. What does the recipient like, appreciate, or enjoy? What message do we wish to convey with the gift? We appreciate you? We thank you? We celebrate this occasion with you?

In the same book, Reid explains that giving has style. The way we give gifts may be as or more important than the gift itself. Think of a time when someone made a special effort in the presentation of the gift to you. Maybe a good friend personally delivered the gift to your house and spent time with you. Maybe you shared a meal and received the gift as part of the sharing. Maybe the note accompanying the gift became the real gift for you. With a little forethought and effort, families can make their delivery of gifts as meaningful as the gifts themselves.

As we consider gift giving, let us also consider gift receiving. Some recipients rip off the paper as fast as they can, make a comment, and race on to the next gift. Some take time to look at the gift and respond, "Oh, I just love this (color, style, brand). I've wanted one of these for so long. Thank you." Some carefully inch off the ribbon, bow, and wrapping paper so it can be reused, paying little attention to the gift itself. Some stack their gifts by their chair and say, "I'll open them later."

How do we receive God's gift of self, Jesus the Christ? Do we glance at the Messiah momentarily, then rush to another gift? Do we study the Christ—how specially Jesus was "wrapped" and "delivered" personally, and at great cost, to us? Do we pause to thank the Giver with our hearts? Or do we focus on the trimmings of the Gift—the mysterious, beautiful story of Jesus' birth, the wonder of the shepherds, the appearance of angels—and miss what Christ's arrival means? Maybe we put off opening the Gift altogether, more interested in the packages under the tree.

As families let us receive the gift of Jesus in love. And then let us receive other gifts as thoughtfully, encouraging each other to be sensitive to the giver. Receiving gifts graciously becomes our gift to the giver.

Much of our gift giving and receiving can be intentional. As we consider who we are, what we have to give, and what the receiver would appreciate, our gifts reflect the giver and the receiver, but most importantly, the Giver of all. These gifts then have potential to become shaping forces in both the giver's and receiver's lives.

HOW WILL PARENTS SHAPE A FAMILY'S GIVING AND RECEIVING?

Parents may unintentionally shape children and youth in the art of giving as they model giving of self. They can intentionally shape their children by consciously being gracious when they receive. My parents practiced both kinds of shaping. We spent the first part of Christmas Eve taking gifts to people who would have less than we would on Christmas. Then we visited aunts, uncles, and others who had touched us during the year. We attended Christmas Eve services. Finally we gathered with my mother's family at my grandparents' home.

There, we kept to the kitchen while the Christmas tree and gifts were being prepared. It was a time of anticipation—and wonderful food. I can still close my eyes and see and taste the delicacies spread on the dining room table: dried deer sausage, chicken salad, cheese, fruitcake, divinity, fudge, pecan pralines, and my favorite drink—a chilled, cooked ice-cream custard.

Finally all the cousins, aunts, and uncles had had their fill of goodies. At last we were allowed to view the sparkling tree surrounded by gaily wrapped gifts. The adults found chairs. Children sat on the floor. My grandparents reminded us, "Not yet!" Singing always came before gifts. We sang both secular songs and sacred Christmas carols. Everybody sang. Sometimes the adults grouped the children and expected us to sing a song of our choice.

The singing of "Silent Night" spoke to us of both *chronos* and *kairos*. We children knew that until we sang "Silent Night," there would be no gift opening. Even in our childlike excitement of the gift opening to come, the singing of this favorite carol brought a hushed holiness over us as we remembered God's gift to us.

On many of those Christmases we knew nothing but the joy of being together. Some Christmases followed a difficult year or the loss of a loved one. On those occasions we sang "Silent Night" with tears streaming down our faces. My family seemed to understand with their heads and their hearts that the ever-present gift of the infant Jesus represented God's love to our family during both good and painful Christmases.

As a young child, I did not understand the visits to friends and relatives on Christmas Eve as choosing *kairos*. I did not appreciate that these visits shaped me in God's image. I did innately understand these family experiences as sharing Christmas love with others. Did my parents intentionally make these visits to shape me in the pattern of God's self-giving love? No—they did it as a response to God's love. But it had a powerful shaping effect in my life. These visits taught me the importance of sharing God's love with others, and that the gift of relationship comes before material gifts.

My family's attendance at Christmas Eve worship reflects both a response to God's love and intentional shaping on their part. As a young child I understood that we always celebrated the gift of Jesus first and then gathered to share family gifts with one another. The gift of Jesus became the focus for Christmas Eve. Intentional shaping!

The tradition of the food and the waiting passed from one generation to another. The first generation of parents made intentional decisions that shaped their children's experience on Christmas Eve. By the time of my childhood, we celebrated as we did because it had always happened that way. Unintentional shaping!

Singing sacred carols just before opening gifts intentionally focused the family on the true meaning of Christmas. The focus on "Silent Night" stilled squiggly children for a holy moment before the tearing of paper began.

The family traditions I experienced on Christmas Eve shaped me in the image of God. Consider how you have been shaped by Christmases past. Whether positive or negative, those memories create a foundation from which to build.

LIVING IN GOD'S TIME:
RECEIVING GOD'S GIFT OF JESUS

Consider the following possibilities for intentionally shaping your family's faith during the Christmas Season. Choose to observe some sacred moments along the *kairos* road.

Preparing the Home Worship Area

Change the purple or royal blue table covering to a white covering. White colors the high holy seasons of Christmas and Easter. Gold trim on the white cloth adds an elegant touch. Remember to have the baby Jesus and the manger to add to the Holy Family. Place the Christ candle in the center of the Advent wreath. Add a cross to your setting, and stand the Advent wreath in front of the cross.

Family Worship Ritual for Christmas Eve/Christmas Day: At the Manger

Leader: *Tonight marks the time known as Christmas Eve (Christmas Day). Tonight marks the end of our waiting for the birth of God's son. Tonight all those who have waited gather at the manger. The prophets gather there. (Light the first purple candle and move the prophet inside the wreath.) Mary and Joseph gather there. (Light the second purple candle and move Mary and Joseph in front of the Christ candle.) The shepherds gather there. (Light the pink candle and move the shepherds beside Mary or Joseph.) The wise men gather there. (Light the third purple candle and move them beside Mary or Joseph.) We gather there.*

Reader: Read the story of the birth of Jesus in the Gospel of Luke 2:1-7.

Leader: *To help us celebrate the gift of God's son, Jesus, we light the Christ candle.* (Light the white candle and place the baby and manger between Mary and Joseph). *Let us enjoy the light of the Christ candle as we think about that holy night.* (Allow for silence before anyone responds to each "I wonder" statement.)

- *I wonder how it would feel to hold the infant Jesus.*
- *I wonder why people say Jesus is our greatest gift of all.*
- *I wonder why the wise men brought gifts to baby Jesus.*
- *I wonder why we give gifts to people we love at Christmas.*
- *I wonder what gift we could give the baby Jesus.*

Prayer: *Most gracious God, we give thanks for the gift of your son, Jesus. Through Jesus, you gifted us with your great love. May our giving and receiving of Christmas gifts reflect your love. Amen.*

Leader: As the assigned person extinguishes the purple and pink candles, say, *We extinguish the light of all those gathered at the manger: the light of the prophets, the light of the Holy Family, the light of the shepherds, and the light of the wise men. Watch while we change the light of Jesus.* (Extinguish the Christ candle.) *Now the light lives in all of God's creation. Now the light lives in our hearts and the hearts of all God's people.*

Weekly Family Worship Ritual for the Sundays of the Christmas Season
(Except Christmas Eve or Day)

Leader: *Today marks a Sunday of the Christmas Season. As God's people we continue to celebrate the mystery of Christmas, the mystery of God coming to walk this earth in the person of Jesus. We remember God's love-gift to us. We continue to give gifts to people we love.*

Reader: Read what the writer of the Gospel of John 1:1-5, 14-18 has to say about how God the Word became God the human.

Leader: *Today we light the Christ candle to remember God's gift to us of Jesus. Let us enjoy the light of Christ that lives in our hearts.* (Allow for silence before anyone responds to each "I wonder" statement.)

- *I wonder how the Word became flesh.*
- *I wonder how long Jesus has been part of God.*
- *I wonder what the Bible means when it says "the Word was God."*

Prayer: *Most loving God, we give you thanks for the gift of your son, Jesus. We know that the light of Jesus lives in our hearts and brings light to our sorrows, our joys, our pain, our work, our play, and our relationships. May our lives reflect the light of Jesus. Amen.*

Leader: As the assigned person extinguishes the Christ candle, say, *Watch while we change the light of Jesus. Now the light lives in all of God's creation. Now the light lives in our hearts and the hearts of all God's people.*

Activities

1. In the Jewish tradition during the Passover meal, the youngest child asks, "Why is this night different from all other nights?" Let's ask this same question about our Christmas celebration. Discuss it one evening as you continue the celebration of Christmas.

2. Read *The Velveteen Rabbit* by Margery Williams and discuss the greatest gift of all. The family may choose to do this as part of their Weekly Family Worship Ritual during the Christmas Season.

Family Reflection on the Season
(Note: Hold your Advent and Christmas reflections at the same time. Have the session early in January before losing the impact of the season.) Discuss:

- How did our family focus on the gift of Jesus?
- What did we hope for this Christmas?
- What gift did we receive from Christmas this year?
- Share the best and worst Christmas gifts received. Did either of these gifts reflect "the gift of self"?
- Did we experience *kairos*, a slowing and silencing of family life when we could draw inward and closer to God?
- Agree to limit the number of gifts given next year. Consider what gifts of self you can substitute for other gifts.
- As parents, consider: did discussions and meditation time help relieve fears?

Shaped by a Different Way Home: Epiphany of the Lord and Ordinary Time I

A s we study the map of life, we plot our course and plan special events, like occupational changes and the births of children. John and Connie spent much time planning, discussing, and marking their map. They smiled in remembrance as they looked at the dot marking the arrival of their infant daughter, Alexandra, from Korea. Now, two years later, they marked the arrival of their second infant, Joshua, also from Korea. They felt this addition completed their family. The map noted John's plan to make a major career change in the next few months. Connie looked at the dot representing her anticipated promotion to the position of special education director. They both smiled at their clearly marked route home. This map would be the intentionally shaping force in their lives.

Joshua had yet to celebrate his first month in his new home when Connie received a call from the adoption agency. "Your daughter's birth parents have another baby to place. We want you to have the first option to adopt."

John and Connie reacted immediately: "He's our baby!" Connie remembered her prayers for Alexandra, how she hoped the baby would have a birth sibling. She also thought of the old adage, "Be careful what you pray for. You may get it!"

But the couple's life map had seemed complete with the addition of Joshua. Questions flooded their minds. As midlife parents, could they manage another child? With her new, more time-consuming job, would Connie have time to care for another infant? And then there was John's upcoming career change to consider.

Family members who heard the news readily remarked that a third child did not make sense according to the life map John and Connie had plotted. They discouraged the adoption and affirmed the couple's previous plans.

A crossroads of life! Which route should they take, the one they planned or a different and uncharted one? For a month John and Connie sat on the fence. Their hearts called them to take the unexpected route home. Common sense, and concerned friends and family, told them to hold steady to their mapped course. Connie often stood outside their house, looking at the sky and asking, "Is God talking to me, or am I talking to me?" She and John wavered between feeling that this baby belonged in their home and that they could never afford—financially and emotionally—to adopt him.

Finally, sensibility seemingly prevailed. Connie and John opted for the plans they had laid. Yet when the agency called and asked for a written decision, Connie waited two weeks before writing the letter. With tears streaming down her face, she finally put on paper their decision to hold steady to their mapped course. She folded the letter and sealed the envelope, but she could not bring herself to mail it. She left it for John to handle.

Connie's maternity leave with Joshua ended and she returned to work. A friend greeted her. As they talked, a realization formed in Connie's mind. Her forty-year-old friend's family included three children with twins soon to arrive. She managed. Suddenly, Connie knew: *I can do this, too!* She called John at work and asked, "Did you put the letter in the mailbox?"

John responded simply, "Yes."

"Can you get it out?"

"I can't possibly be there by the 11:30 mail delivery time."

"Well, call the neighbors!" urged Connie. "Maybe someone didn't go to work today."

John didn't argue. He began calling the neighbors, all of whom worked outside the home. Unbelievably, he reached a neighbor home with a sick child. John asked, "Has the mailman come today?"

The neighbor responded, "I don't know. I can go see."

"Please do! And if he hasn't come, please take the letter out of our mailbox!" John said.

The neighbor soon called, saying she had retrieved the letter—the postal carrier had been late. John then called the agency. The director informed him that the baby had been assigned over the weekend. John was shaken by the news. He knew that once the agency met with a family, no changes would be made. He called Connie to tell her. They agreed that if the baby had been assigned, the map need not be changed. A sinking feeling enveloped Connie.

When they arrived home late one evening, a message on their answering machine said an emergency had prevented the assigned family from meeting with the agency. The recording ended, "Call me." John and Connie called the director and said, "He's ours! Start the paperwork!" God's light marked the different path.

To accommodate the new arrival, Connie declined her promotion and asked instead for a year's leave from her present job. John waited several more years to make a career change. They borrowed money to adopt, called their surprised families, and said, "He'll be here in June!" Both felt deep relief as they responded to God's call to take the baby. Traveling this uncharted route home, they knew their lives would never be the same, but they felt utter peace in their decision.

AN HISTORICAL SURPRISE ROUTE

Some two thousand years ago some other people experienced an unexpected route home. The wise men who followed a star's light in search of a baby set people to wondering. Who was this child they were seeking? Even King Herod, in great distress, wondered, "Could this child be the one to rule God's people Israel?" He instructed the wise men to tell him of their findings when they returned.

We know the wise men found the baby in Bethlehem and that they knelt in adoration, offering their gifts to the infant King. In a dream an angel told the wise men of King Herod's intent to harm the child and warned them to take another way home. The glad tidings of Christmas traveled with the wise men as they followed the different route.

We celebrate the Epiphany of the Lord, the manifestation of Christ to the world, on January 6. On this date we believe the wise men arrived at the stable in Bethlehem. This event culminates the celebration of the mystery of Christmas and the Christmas Season. Following the Epiphany of the Lord, we begin the Season after the Epiphany (Ordinary Time I). Here we celebrate God's call to take different paths, and the effect our obedience has on those with whom we come in contact. God wants our obedience to let others know of Christ.

A second Epiphany story also describes an historical surprise route and invites us to take the unexpected way home. The story of Jesus' baptism on the first Sunday after the Epiphany of the Lord calls us to not only remember the Christ's baptism but also to remember our own. Baptized in the river Jordan, Jesus, according to the Gospel of Matthew, retreated immediately into the desert to struggle with what it meant to be identified as the son of God. There in the desert, the newly baptized Jesus had to choose between the road the tempter offered or God's different road. Likewise, our baptism identifies us as sons and daughters of God. As baptized children we too must choose whether to follow the call of the world or the call of God.

MY—AND YOUR—LIFE MAP

As marked on my own life map, the Reverend C. R. Brewster poured the baptismal waters over my head and identified me as a child of God. The family of faith present at my baptism nurtured and loved me along my faith journey. One of the ways they did this was to make sure we never missed Sunday school. Thus, it seemed strange to me, a number of years later, that I could not name a Sunday school teacher who changed my life. I have heard many other persons name a special teacher who influenced or changed their lives. Then one day the truth dawned on me. I cannot name that one teacher because my parents taught me the most about our faith. Daily they lived their beliefs: Love God first. Love God first by being present in worship, by serving in many capacities within the life of the church, by understanding that possessions and abilities came as gifts from God, by being faithful to the church of Jesus Christ even when that church makes decisions you disagree with or the pastor is not to your liking. God has claimed us as God's people and, in response, we love God first.

My childhood years followed a clearly marked route on my map of life. Yet God's call to the uncharted route came often. Though I expected to experience marriage and motherhood, I wasn't prepared for the other, unusual directions my life would take: teaching in public school, becoming certified as a Christian educator, ministry that took me for years at a time to different cities, single motherhood, and now, authoring a book. Changes, surprises, struggle—and joy—all mark God's call to take another way home.

My journey, and yours, is like that of the wise men. We are often called to a path whose consequences are unclear. Did the wise men understand that their obedience to God's warning kept the infant Jesus safe from King Herod? Did John and Connie fully comprehend what their decision to adopt the new infant would mean? Have I always known where my choice to follow God would lead? No.

The wise men, John and Connie, and I all listened and heard God's call in the midst of everyday life—in a dream, through the tardiness of a postal worker, and, in my case, through startling phone calls. Neither the wise men, John and Connie, nor I knew the changes we would experience in our lives or the way in which God would use us. But God practiced intentional shaping; so did we when we said yes to God's different and uncharted way home. We must trust God for the shape our lives will take as we follow God's call.

The Season after the Epiphany calls families to look at their life maps. Can we see God in the everydayness of our lives? Can we help our children to plan short-term life maps, staying open to God's call to take paths different from those they planned? To journey with God we must be willing to travel this road, realizing that God may never reveal to us the reason for the different and uncharted route home.

LIVING IN GOD'S TIME:
CHOOSING TO TRAVEL THE DIFFERENT AND
UNCHARTED ROUTE

Preparing the Home Worship Area

Keep the white cloth of the Christmas Season for January 6 and the first Sunday in the Season after the Epiphany, the Baptism of the Lord. Following these two dates, change the white cloth to a green covering for the remainder of the Season after the Epiphany (Ordinary Time I).

Remove the Advent wreath. Stand the Christ candle in front of the cross. In front of the candle, place a gold crown around the Holy Family figures. The crown and figures symbolize the world's knowledge that Jesus' birth fulfills the prophecies of the long-awaited Messiah.

Weekly Family Worship Ritual for the Epiphany

Leader: *Today marks the Epiphany of the Lord. We celebrate the wise men taking the different route home. We remember how their willingness to travel this route kept Jesus safe from King Herod. We remember how God identified Jesus as God's son in baptism. God claims us in baptism and calls us to take the different and uncharted route home.*

Reader: Read the story of the wise men from the Gospel of Matthew 2:1-12.

Leader: *God became human in Jesus. Jesus taught people. Jesus healed people. They questioned, "Who are you?" And Jesus said, "I am the light that lives in the hearts of God's people." Let us enjoy the light of Christ who lives in our hearts as we continue to wonder.* (Light the Christ candle. Allow for silence before anyone responds to each "I wonder" statement.)

61

• *I wonder if you can think of a time you took a different and uncharted route home.*

• *I wonder what might have happened if the wise men had reported back to King Herod.*

• *I wonder how their decision not to do that affects us today.*

• *I wonder why God calls people to take different routes home.*

• *I wonder if you can think of times as you grow up that God might call you to take a different route home.* (Note: This will depend on the ages of your children, but have them consider the pressures of the world they will face: drugs, alcohol, peer pressure, cheating, being unkind.)

Prayer: *God, you called the wise men to take a different road home. You call us to do the same. May we travel with courage. Amen.*

Leader: As the assigned person extinguishes the candle, say, *Watch while we change the light of Jesus. Now the light lives in all of God's creation. Now the light lives in our hearts and in the hearts of all God's people.*

Weekly Family Worship Ritual for the First Sunday in the Season
after the Epiphany (Ordinary Time I)

Leader: *Today marks the first Sunday after the Epiphany. We celebrate the wise men taking the different route home. We remember how their willingness to travel this route kept Jesus safe from King Herod. We remember how God identified Jesus as God's son in baptism. God claims us in baptism and calls us to take the different route home.*

Reader: Read the baptism of Jesus according to the Gospel of Luke 3:21-22.

Leader: *God became human in Jesus. Jesus taught people. Jesus healed people. They questioned, "Who are you?" And Jesus said, "I am the light that lives in the hearts of God's people." Let us enjoy the light of Christ who lives in our hearts as we continue to wonder.* (Light the Christ candle. Allow for silence before anyone responds to each "I wonder" statement.)

- *I wonder why it is important to be baptized.*
- *I wonder what sign God gave to show God claimed Jesus in baptism.*
- *I wonder how you would answer if you were asked who Jesus is.*

Prayer: *Gracious God, you marked us with water and claimed us as your own. We are your children and you are our God. Help us to live as your children. Amen.*

Leader: As the assigned person extinguishes the candle, say, *Watch while we change the light of Jesus. Now the light lives in all of God's creation. Now the light lives in our hearts and the hearts of all God's people.*

Weekly Family Worship Ritual for the Second Sunday after the Epiphany
Leader: *Today marks the second Sunday after the Epiphany. We celebrate the wise men taking the different route home. We remember how their willingness to travel this route kept Jesus safe from King Herod. We remember how God identified Jesus as God's son in baptism. God claims us in baptism and calls us to take the different route home.*

Reader: Read the story of the wedding at Cana in the Gospel of John 2:1-11.

Leader: *God became human in Jesus. Jesus taught people. Jesus healed people. They questioned, "Who are you?" And Jesus said, "I am the light that lives in the hearts of God's people." Let us enjoy the light of Christ who lives in our hearts as we continue to think about that festive day.* (Light the Christ candle. Allow for silence before anyone responds to each "I wonder" statement.)

• *I wonder why Jesus turned water into wine at a wedding feast.*

• *I wonder why Jesus ordered the best wine served at the end of the wedding when usually the bridegroom served it early.*

• *I wonder what Mary expected to happen.*

Prayer: *Gracious God, help us to live as followers of the light. At work, at school, or at play, help us to look for ways we can share your light with those around us. Amen.*

Leader: As the assigned person extinguishes the candle, say, *Watch while we change the light of Jesus. Now the light lives in all of God's creation. Now the light lives in our hearts and the hearts of all God's people.*

Weekly Family Worship Ritual for the Other Sundays in the Season after the Epiphany (Ordinary Time I)

Leader: *Today marks a Sunday in the Season after the Epiphany. We celebrate the wise men taking the different route home. We remember how their willingness to travel this route kept Jesus safe from King Herod. We remember how God identified Jesus as God's son in baptism. God claims us in baptism and calls us to take the different route home.*

Reader: Reread the stories of the first three Sundays or read about Jesus as a boy in Luke 2:41-52, the temptations Jesus faced in Luke 4:1-13, or Jesus' rejection at Nazareth in Luke 4:16-30.

Leader: *God became human in Jesus. Jesus taught people. Jesus healed people. They questioned, "Who are you?" And Jesus said, "I am the light that lives in the hearts of God's people." Let us enjoy the light of Christ who lives in our hearts as we continue to wonder.* (Light the Christ candle. Allow for silence before anyone responds to each "I wonder" statement.)

- *I wonder why Jesus stayed behind in Jerusalem.*
- *I wonder what tempts you.*
- *I wonder why the people drove Jesus out of his hometown.*

Prayer: *Gracious God, help us to live as followers of the light. At work, at school, or at play, help us to look for ways we can share your light with those around us. Amen.*

Leader: As the assigned person extinguishes the candle, say, *Watch while we change the light of Jesus. Now the light lives in all of God's creation. Now the light lives in our hearts and the hearts of all God's people.*

Activities

1. If your church does not host an Epiphany celebration, prepare one for your home. This is called the Feast of the Three Kings. Make the traditional bean cake (your favorite bundt-cake recipe will do). Plant three beans, representing the wise men, inside the cake. (If your family has fewer than three children, plant just one bean.) Crown the persons who find the beans as the wise ones of your home for twenty-four hours. The wise ones have the privilege of making some minor family decisions for the period of their reign. They might choose the menu, declare a family activity, or assign a family member to be a star-bearer in a retelling of the story of the wise men. In this activity, the wise ones lead the family in following the star-bearer through the house and discussing what the journey might have been like. The family reenactment concludes at the nativity set, where the gold crowns are placed. (This would be a good time to do the Weekly Family Worship Ritual for the Epiphany.)

2. Particularly during the season of Epiphany, look for opportunities to encourage your children to listen for God's call to take another way home. For example, instead of saying to children, "That's a bad choice" or "In this family we don't tell lies," you might say, "The wise men had to make a choice. They had to choose which way to go home. King Herod had told the wise men to travel through Jerusalem on their way home so they could tell him about the new king. God called them to take a different route home. Today you had a choice. I heard you call Suzie a bad name. What else could you have said? Which would God want you to choose?" This statement asks children to consider their actions in light of the story of the three wise men. Then a disciplinary issue holds the potential for becoming an epiphany, intentionally shaping faith.

Family Reflection on the Season

Take time to discuss as a family your celebration of the Epiphany of the Lord and the Season after the Epiphany.

- During this season, did we take a different road home?
- What part of our celebration would we like to keep for next year? What would we like to change?
- Close with this statement: "I wonder why we celebrate Epiphany." Be silent for a few moments as the children think about their answers.

Shaped by the Distance from the Head to the Heart: Lent

For forty days and nights, Noah waited with his family and God's creatures in the ark for deliverance from the floodwaters. For forty years the Israelites wandered in the wilderness, waiting to enter the Promised Land. Jesus spent forty days in the desert, struggling for definition in ministry.

How shall we travel through the season of Lent? How shall we make this forty-day journey from the head to the heart? For what shall we wait, hope, and struggle in the path toward Easter? We can learn much from a little girl named Hannah, who with childlike wonder lived from her heart.

Hannah, a first grader, had spent all of her six years in the same church. Her parents, two sisters, and maternal grandparents were also part of her church family. Many described Betsy, the grandmother, as one of the "saints" of the church because of her many gifts and the way she used them. Betsy loved to talk—for the Lord, that is. She taught youth Sunday school classes for years. And she did more than teach—she wrote notes to the students when they were absent and phoned to tell them she missed them. In the church at large, she spoke out in meetings. She trained to be a speaker and spoke at her home church and in others. She taught an adult Bible study for two years. She gave notes of appreciation to the staff and verbally blessed them for their leadership.

In short, Betsy used all of her energy—and her vocal cords—to serve the Lord and the Lord's people. We all came to love and appreciate her.

One January, Betsy developed a persistent hoarseness. Over the months her condition worsened. The muscles in her face and throat began to weaken and speech became difficult. The next year I finished teaching her adult Bible class. Time brought no improvement in her conditions. Speaking became more difficult with each passing day. Disease had now taken from her the very thing she loved to do most: use her voice for the Lord.

Our church gathered weekly to share a meal and to pray. On one particular Tuesday evening, I saw Hannah, the youngest of Betsy's five granddaughters, tug on her mother's hand. Hannah's mother tried to get Hannah to offer her own prayer. But Hannah kept asking her mother, "You say it for me." Finally her mother said, "Hannah wants to pray for NaNa." Over the weeks, as Betsy's speech difficulties increased and her ability to eat lessened, Hannah continued to insist that her mother ask us to pray for NaNa.

Months later, Betsy could no longer speak at all. She carried a note pad and wrote her messages to us. She lived on a liquid diet and steadily lost weight. One Sunday, Hannah, her older sisters, and her mother came up to me after church. The mother handed me a folded bulletin and said, "Hannah wrote you a note." The mother and I went on talking as I held the note.

Suddenly I felt the Holy Spirit nudge me. I said, "Hannah, do you want me to read the note now?" Hannah shook her head yes. So I opened the note and in a first grader's printing it read, "Please pray for NaNa." I assured Hannah that we would and went on talking with her Mother.

The Holy Spirit nudged me again. I looked at the little girl. "Hannah," I said, "does this note mean you want the pastors and me to pray for NaNa in our daily prayers, or does it mean you want us to pray out loud for NaNa in church?"

"Pray out loud in church," she responded.

Betsy had requested that during her illness her name not appear on the prayer list in the bulletin nor be spoken during the worship service. Like any true saint, she wanted no special attention. But at the next church meeting, I sat by Betsy and said, "One of your very special granddaughters wrote me a note that I think you would appreciate." I showed her the note. "Do you know which one wrote it?" She nodded. I told her of the request Hannah had made and asked Betsy if we could pray aloud for her in worship. She smiled—yes.

The Sunday dawned for the offering of this prayer. Hannah's mother stopped in the hall to tell me that all week Hannah had been very excited. She could hardly wait until Sunday, because on that day we would pray for NaNa. Hannah had awakened bright and early that morning. She urged the family to hurry and get ready for Sunday school and church. Besides carrying anticipation for the prayer for NaNa, Hannah carried with her a cereal bowl full of nickels, dimes, and quarters to give to the church for the poor.

We did pray for Betsy on that Sunday, and on many following Sundays. Unfortunately, we learned later, her condition was terminal. She died the following November—on Thanksgiving morning!

The news of her death reached me in my hometown on Thanksgiving

Day. I called Hannah's mom to express my love. She relayed the story of the last days. It seems that when the doctors told the family that they thought the end was near, their grief became tears. Hannah told them, "Stop crying. You'll make me cry! Besides, whatever is going to happen, it will be all right."

Blond-haired, blue-eyed Hannah, a first grader, exemplifies for us how to live in our Lenten journey. When crisis entered her life, she responded from her heart with great spiritual strength. She unknowingly modeled Jesus as she prayed, practiced almsgiving, and made difficult decisions.

LENT: PRAY, GIVE, DECIDE, FAST

During the forty days of Lent, we enter our own desert time, penitentially considering our Christlikeness. This liturgical season calls us to go intentionally inward to see if our lives reflect the life of Jesus. We examine our behavior in light of our intellectual understandings of faith. We make our goal to live from our hearts more clearly what we know with our heads. We prepare for the great mystery of Easter with an intensity of introspection. We shape our lives more intentionally after the example of Jesus by praying, fasting, almsgiving, and making tough decisions.

First is praying without ceasing. Jesus teaches about this kind of prayer in the parable of the widow in Luke 18:1-8: "God, whether you will or whether you will not, I will not let you alone" (AP). Hannah modeled that as she persistently prayed on behalf of her "NaNa."

Prayer links us in communication to God. Listening and speaking comprise good communication. Sometimes we think of prayer as only talking to God. We forget to practice a time of silence in which we can also listen for God.

Praying without ceasing means we pray prayers of thanksgiving even when it's difficult. We lift up our eyes to the hills and remember the Creator with praise. We give thanks for all that God has given us even when the pain of our lives almost blots out the goodness. And when things are going smoothly, we remember to thank God for that, too!

It means we tell God what hides in our hearts: fear, anger, hurt, and doubt. We find it easy to tell our best friend these things. Do we not know our God to be bigger than our best friend?

It means we pray while we do other things. We go to the office. We clean the house. We take care of other people.

Praying without ceasing means we trust God enough to invite God into every area of our lives. Trusting that God will be faithful, we lean, let go, and leap. We rely on God's reign even in the moments of pain. We do not know when God will answer our prayers. We do not know if God will answer the way we hope or the way we need—and we often don't know the difference. But our constant prayer shows we trust our God's faithfulness, and it moves us closer to Christlikeness.

Giving reflects another means of moving from head to heart. Hannah practiced giving by collecting change for the poor. She remembered to carry this offering to church when her grandmother was ill and prayers for her were a priority. Even in Hannah's concern for her grandmother, her heart reached toward people who had less materially than she had.

The Bible often refers to sharing material gifts as almsgiving. In its truest sense, almsgiving means giving from a thankful heart to those in need. According to the Gospel of Luke, we know that Jesus spent the most time serving the least, the last, and the lost. The gift of money is one means of help, but families can serve others in more meaningful ways. Youth and children's mission trips and activities sponsored by a congregation provide ways for children and youth to serve others. In serving others, we find ourselves shaped by those whom we serve as well as by the experience of serving. Helping others moves us from the head to the heart as we seek to follow Jesus.

A third spiritual practice is making difficult decisions. Decision making moves us from being philosophers and dreamers to becoming people of action—people who get things changed and accomplished. Hannah made several important and often difficult decisions: she chose to follow Christ, even when she didn't understand Christ's allowing her beloved grandmother to experience illness. She chose to give to others in the midst of her concern. She chose to seek public prayers on behalf of Betsy, even though fear caused her to speak through her mom. And in the end, she chose to believe in God's reign despite evidence to the contrary: she knew Betsy would be all right even in death.

Difficult decision making comes with living life—and with choosing to be shaped in God's image. The temptation to keep living from the head instead of learning to live from the heart during Lent calls us to make difficult decisions. We can proceed through the Lenten season by asking in each dilemma, "What would Jesus do?"

Maybe we should all practice the ritual of reckoning described in Robert Fulghum's book *From Beginning to End: The Rituals of Our Lives.* Maybe we should be like the man in one of the book's photos who sits upon his own cemetery plot contemplating his life and his death. Maybe we should make the first morning look in the mirror a ritual of reckoning. What if each morning when we looked in the mirror we knew exactly the number of days we had left to live? Would we not find it easier to resist the temptation of the world and to follow Jesus? Would we not find it easier to live from the heart?

Jesus spent forty days in the desert, struggling for definition of ministry.

We have at least forty days each year to spend time with our God in the desert, wrestling with and resolving difficult decisions.

A fourth discipline that deepens our Lenten journey is fasting. I don't know if Hannah fasted, but its power has been demonstrated in other lives. Originally, fasting meant the act of self-denial in which persons abstained from meat or other foods. With the termination of fasting as a part of church law, many people discontinued the practice altogether. In the modern world, fasting became a means of self-indulgence rather than self-denial as people used the period of Lenten fasting to diet. In the postmodern era, fasting means to give up self in service to a larger truth. We reinvest the money and time we save through fasting to help others.

Fasting might mean giving up meetings or activities during Lent in order to spend time with God or with family. In whatever sacrifice we make, we move from a head-driven living to a heart-driven spirituality .

LIVING IN GOD'S TIME: SHAPED BY THE DISTANCE FROM THE HEAD TO THE HEART

How do we incorporate praying, almsgiving, making difficult decisions, and fasting into the Lenten journey from the head to the heart? How do we shape our lives more meaningfully after the example of Jesus? Consider these suggestions for your family.

Preparing the Home Worship Area

Change the green cloth of the Season after the Epiphany to a purple cloth for Lent. We use purple because during Lent we prepare to celebrate the mystery of Easter. Purple signifies the royalty of Jesus and the penitential tone of the season. Hang a crown of thorns on the cross. Place the Christ candle in front of the cross. Place an open Bible in front of the Christ candle.

Lent begins on the day designated as Ash Wednesday. Many churches have services on this day and your family may choose to participate in such a service. The burning of last year's palm branches provides the ashes to be used in the liturgy of the day. Usually the priest or minister dips a thumb into the ashes, then marks a cross on the forehead of the believer, saying, "Repent, and believe in the gospel." For young children some pastors say, "Believe in Jesus, follow Jesus." The cross on our foreheads makes a statement to the world that we want to be like Jesus. With proper explanation, three- and four-year-olds will be comfortable participating in these services. If your church does not have such a service, then create your own home service.

Family Worship Ritual for Ash Wednesday

Leader: *Today marks the beginning of the season of Lent. Today we begin remembering Jesus' journey to the cross. Today we begin our journey from our head to our heart. As we begin our journey, each of you write or draw on a piece of paper how you want to be more like Jesus.* (Allow time for family members to do this. Help the younger ones to think of ways they can be more like Jesus. Be specific. "I can be more loving like Jesus by _____.")

Place the pieces of paper in a container or the fireplace. Burn them. When the ashes have cooled, use them to mark the sign of the cross on each person's forehead, saying, *Believe in Jesus, follow Jesus.*

Reader: Read Joel 2:12-18 and/or Matthew 6:1-6, or 6:6-18.

Leader: *God became human in Jesus. Jesus taught people. Jesus healed people. They questioned, "Who are you?" And Jesus said, "I am the light that lives in the hearts of God's people." Let us enjoy the light of the Christ who lives in our hearts as we continue to wonder.* (Light the Christ candle. Allow for silence before anyone responds to each "I wonder" statement.)

- *I wonder why the Lord says, "Return to me with all your heart" and not "Return to me with all your mind."*
- *I wonder what it means to "rend your heart."*
- *I wonder why Jesus tells us to fast, pray, and give alms in secret.*
- *I wonder why we mark our foreheads with a cross at the beginning of Lent.*

Prayer: *Most gracious God, help us to keep our eyes upon Jesus during this forty days of Lent. Help us to follow Jesus, learning to live from the heart what we know with our heads. Strengthen us in our commitment to fast, pray, give alms, and make difficult decisions during these forty days. Amen.*

Leader: As the assigned person extinguishes the light, say, *Watch while we change the light of Jesus. Now the light lives in all of God's creation. Now the light lives in our hearts and the hearts of all God's people.*

Weekly Family Worship Ritual for the First Five Sundays of Lent
Leader: *Today marks the first* (second, third, and so on) *Sunday of Lent. Today we begin remembering Jesus' journey to the cross as we prepare for the great mystery of Easter. Today we begin our journey from our head to our heart. Today let us simplify our lifestyle like Jesus and spend time with our God by praying, fasting, giving alms, and making difficult decisions.*

Reader: Use the scripture readings provided in the lectionary your church uses or these:
First Sunday: Matthew 4:1-11
Second Sunday: John 3:1-17

Third Sunday: John 4:5-42

Fourth Sunday: Luke 15:1-3, 11-32

Fifth Sunday: John 12:20-33

Leader: *God became human in Jesus. Jesus taught people. Jesus healed people. They questioned, "Who are you?" And Jesus said, "I am the light that lives in the hearts of God's people."* Let us enjoy the light of the Christ who lives in our hearts as we continue to wonder. (Light the Christ candle. Allow for silence before anyone responds to each "I wonder" statement.)

(Below are some questions that may be applied to the scripture readings for each of the five Sundays. Make up some of your own that apply to that particular story.)

- *I wonder how we can be like Jesus in this story.*
- *I wonder what this story tells us about living from the heart.*
- *I wonder what this story tells us about the mystery of Easter.*
- *I wonder what you wonder about this story.*

Prayer: *Most gracious God, help us to keep our eyes upon Jesus during this forty days of Lent. Help us to follow Jesus and learn to live from the heart what we know with our heads. Strengthen us in our commitment to pray, give alms, make difficult decisions, and fast during these forty days.*

Leader: While the assigned person extinguishes the candle, say, *Watch while we change the light of Jesus. Now the light lives in all of God's creation. Now the light lives in our hearts and the hearts of all God's people.*

Weekly Family Worship Ritual for Holy Week

Holy Week begins with Palm Sunday, the sixth Sunday of Lent or the Sunday before Easter. The week intensifies as we follow Jesus through his last days. Many churches have special observances throughout the week. Decide in which ones your family will participate and what you wish to do at home during this week.

One option would be to read and/or reenact the scriptures corresponding to Jesus' life each day of this week. You may wish to set a candelabra that holds seven purple candles in front of the Christ candle. On Palm Sunday, light all seven candles after reading the passage for the day. Thereafter, light one candle less for each day of the week. On Saturday there will be total darkness. During Advent we add light each week as we prepare to receive the light of Christ; during Holy Week we extinguish the light as we remember how we participated in the darkness of Jesus' life.

Leader: *This week marks the last days of Jesus' life. Each day we take time to walk the way of the cross with Jesus. We remember that people like us took Jesus' life. We remember that people like us betrayed Jesus. We remember that people like us went into hiding out of fear.*

Reader: From the chart below read the scripture for the appropriate day. Dramatize the reading if you wish.

DAY	EVENT	SCRIPTURE
Palm Sunday	Entry Into Jerusalem	Matthew 21:1-11

You will need palm branches or some similar plant to wave and place on your family worship area.

DAY	EVENT	SCRIPTURE
Monday	Jesus in the Temple	Mark 11:15-19
Tuesday	Jesus Teaches	Mark 12:28-34
Wednesday	Jesus Anointed	Mark 14:3-9
Maundy Thursday	The Last Supper	Matthew 26:17-30

This is a good evening to celebrate a Christian paschal meal, which connects the Passover seder supper with the institution of the sacrament of Holy Communion. You can purchase a booklet at your Christian bookstore that will lead the family through such a celebration. At the conclusion of this service and in preparation for Good Friday, extinguish all the purple candles and remove everything from the family worship area except the Christ candle.

Good Friday	Jesus' Crucifixion	Matthew 27:27-61

Extinguish the Christ candle when you read in the scripture that Jesus died. Close the Bible at the end of your family worship and remove everything from the family worship area. This day should be quiet and solemn.

Holy Saturday	Disciples Mourn	Luke 23:50-56

Read the Easter chapter of this book to determine the necessary preparations that need to be made on this day.

Leader: *God became human in Jesus. Jesus taught people. Jesus healed people. They questioned, "Who are you?" And Jesus said, "I am the light that lives in the hearts of God's people."* (Light the Christ candle.) *We light these other candles as reminders of the light of Christ that lives in God's people.* (Light the appropriate number of candles.) *Let us enjoy the light of the Christ who lives in our hearts as we continue to wonder.* (Allow for silence before anyone responds to each "I wonder" statement.)

- *I wonder how Jesus felt these last days of Jesus' life.*
- *I wonder how the disciples felt.*
- *I wonder how Jesus' mother felt.*
- *I wonder whom you would have been most like during these last days of Jesus' life.*

Prayer: *O God, help us to have the courage to walk all the way to the cross with Jesus. We hope that we would have been with the women at the foot of the cross and not in hiding with the disciples or laughing and jeering with the soldiers. You did not desert your son. You will not desert us. Amen.*

Leader: As the assigned person extinguishes the candles, say, *Watch while we change the light of Jesus. Now the light lives in all of God's creation. Now the light lives in our hearts and the hearts of all God's people.*

Activities

1. As the weather begins to warm, try "walking prayers." As a family, take a walk. When someone sees something to pray for, pause and offer a sentence prayer.

2. Encourage your family to fast, to give up something in order to spend time together making this Lenten journey.
   - Give up a television program the first week, and add an additional program each week of Lent. Remember to use the time to be with God and the family.

• For whatever you give up during Lent, fill yourself with God's Word. Read the Gospel of Mark or the Psalms.

• If you choose to give up a meal, fast foods, or desserts, put the money saved at each simplified meal in a bowl. At the end of Lent donate the money to an agency that feeds the homeless.

Family Reflection on the Season

Discuss as a family:

• What part of our Lenten observation did you find most meaningful?

• Were you more prepared to celebrate the mystery of Easter? Why?

• How did our family's Lenten activities move us from our heads to our hearts?

• How did we focus more on living like Jesus?

• What did we do during this season that we want to do again next year? What new things might we add to our period of preparation?

Shaped By Water (Resurrection): Easter Season

☙

For years, prophets warned Judah that if she did not mend her ways she would fall into the hands of a stronger power. As Babylon stood knocking on the door, King Zedekiah sent for the prophet Jeremiah and inquired, "Is there any word from the LORD?" (Jer. 37:17)

Previously the Israelites had waited four hundred years as slaves in Egypt. They had wondered then, "Is there any word from the Lord?"

After their deliverance from Egypt, God's people wandered forty years in the desert. Not surprisingly, they questioned, "Is there any word from the Lord?"

Now we have waited forty days during our Lenten preparation. Like the Israelites, we ask, "Is there any word from the Lord?"

As Jeremiah answered King Zedekiah, "There is!"

From the empty tomb, God's Word speaks: *The risen Christ lives on this Easter Day.* By human hands Jesus died. By God's action, Jesus lives. God parted the waters of the Red Sea to lead the Israelites from slavery to freedom. God led the people through the waters of the river Jordan into the Promised Land. God delivers us through the baptismal waters into new life with Christ.

Water is a crucial element in the journey we make from head to heart, because this journey begins with our baptism. The baptismal waters offer us continued refreshment as we struggle to live from our hearts like Jesus. They plant deep within us seeds of resurrection that can grow into new life in times of death. Writer Don Saliers says, "We are all journeying; we are all growing toward that which has been conferred by water and the Spirit."[1]

The contemporary church has reinstated the early Christian practice of setting aside Easter as a day for baptism. Through this practice, history, Word, and sacrament join together in a passage from an old way of life to a new one. With the newly baptized we remember that seeds of resurrection find a nurturing place within us and will grow and flourish. Baptism reminds us that in all death situations, we can find new life.

On Easter Day we celebrate our new birth in Christ by remembering baptism as the outward symbol of God's saving act. We sing of God's restoring love. Persons, events, and our own decisions sometimes shape us in ways that do not reflect the image of God, and move us away from our baptism. Through Jesus Christ, God reminds us of the resurrection waters of our baptism and once again offers to shape us in the image of God.

A CONTEMPORARY SEARCH FOR THE RESURRECTION WATERS

Reverend Bob Huie and Bishop Janice Riggle Huie know what it means to need resurrection waters. In June 1994, their thirteen-year-old son, David, died in a go-cart accident.

Bishop Huie told a congregation of her son's death: "Death, like birth, is a holy mystery. Too many words can diminish it. At Jesus' birth, the mother herself is silent. Angels speak, shepherds speak, Simeon speaks. Mary treasures all these words and ponders them in her heart.

"At Jesus' death, Mary is silent again. At the death of a child, what is left for a mother to say? When the EMS person tried to gently explain to me that one child would go to the hospital, but that there was no need for the other child, David, to go to the hospital because he was already dead, a hole was blown through my soul that went through to eternity."

Bishop Huie waits for resurrection waters—for the Source to bring new life through Christ in the death of her son, David. In her pain and grief, Bishop Huie waits to see and know the healing presence of the resurrected Christ. In one way or another, we all wait for the same presence. As Jesus came to those first disciples, he comes to us. In our midst Jesus stands, saying, "Peace be with you."

He came speaking peace to me in June 1997 as I anticipated my ordination as a permanent deacon of The United Methodist Church. I arrived in Corpus Christi for the Southwest Texas Annual Conference, remembering a deceased friend, Betsy, in whom I had experienced the risen Christ. Betsy could always be counted amongst those in my "cheering section." She had often encouraged me to become ordained. How I wished she could be present at this special time in my life! I still grieved for her presence, her support, and her friendship.

During the opening celebration of Holy Communion, many serving stations offered the elements to the large gathering. As I approached the serving station closest to me to receive the bread and wine in remembrance of Jesus, the server reached for my hand and whispered, "The paten and chalice from which you will receive the elements were given in memory of Betsy." As my fingers touched the chalice, I knew Betsy's presence and the power and the truth of resurrection. And I knew the presence of Christ.

During the Easter Season the church celebrates for fifty days the presence of the risen Christ. Jesus let the disciples see and touch the scars on his body so that they would know and believe in his death and resurrection. As a resurrection people, we may know Christ, but when death comes—that of a loved one, of a relationship, of life's work, of long-held goals, or of good health—we struggle once again to know and believe the *resurrected* Christ in those deaths. Bishop Huie knows Christ in her life, but she must seek to know and believe the resurrected Christ in the death of her son. As Jesus taught the disciples of long ago, so Jesus teaches us to find new life in our losses. The risen Christ knows our grief, experiences our grief with us, and calls us forth to new life.

SPECIAL CONCERNS OF THE EASTER SEASON

Life and death issues often plague children, youth, and even adults during this Easter Season as we strive to make sense out of the mystery of Easter: Jesus died, yet Jesus lives with us. Remember Bishop Huie's words as she spoke of her son's death, "Too many words can diminish it." As you confront these issues with your children, be honest in admitting the things you do not know. Answer only the questions your child really asks, not those you think they are asking. And be sensitive to times you should be silent.

I remember a time my mom and I were visiting in the front seat as I drove through heavy city traffic. Suddenly, from the car seat in the back, my two-year-old son said, "Mom, where do you go when you die?"

My mind began to race. I thought, *Oh no, here's the big question! What do I tell a two-year-old?* I looked over at Mom for help. She said nothing.

So I took a deep breath and started by saying, "We go to heaven to live with God."

"No," said my son, "who digs the hole?"

I smiled in relief. All my son wanted to know at that particular time concerned a practical issue—who digs the grave—not a theological question.

At some point in life almost all of us ask, "Why, God? Why did our loved one have to die?" Here it is important to admit you don't know why. As a fifth grader I asked those questions. My mother's good friend died of cancer, leaving a husband and three young sons in grief. One night as my mother and I had our usual bedtime conversation, I poured out my concern, "Why did Jewel have to die? She's still needed. She hasn't lived her life." I honestly do not remember what my mother told me. But I do remember that she listened. She comforted me. She made room for those baptismal seeds of resurrection planted by God to grow within me. She shaped me, and she allowed God to shape me by giving me room to be with God.

Sometimes children need only space to voice their wonderings and confirmation from a significant adult. Three-year-old Lancy, after experiencing several deaths in the family, had this conversation with her mother:

Lancy: "Uncle Olen's dead."

Mom: "Yes."

Lancy: "Uncle Olen is in heaven."

Mom: "Yes."

Lancy: "God's in heaven."

Mom: "Yes."

Lancy: "Uncle Olen is with God."

Mom: "Yes."

Lancy: "God lives in our heart."

Mom: "Yes."

Lancy: "So, Uncle Olen lives in our heart."

Mom: "Yes."

Lancy: "He's still with us."

Mom: "Yes."

Lancy: "So, why are we sad?"

Lancy appears to work it out all by herself and needs only Mom's affirming "Yes." If you look closely, however, at Lancy's conversation it is apparent that certain language shaping her in the image of God had been intentionally used in her home. Thus Lancy had the answer within herself.

As we cope with all the issues of Easter and of life, the holy waters of baptism and Easter continue to shape us. Each Easter we renew our own vows of baptism, so that the seed of resurrection planted in us will continue to flourish as we live our new lives, claimed and cherished by God. The prophet Jeremiah was right: There is a word from the Lord. Christ is risen! And we continually find new life in Christ's resurrected life!

LIVING IN GOD'S TIME:
EXPERIENCING THE RESURRECTION WATERS

Preparing the Home Worship Area

Rebuild the family worship area with a white cloth. Replace the symbols of Lent with symbols of Easter. Remove the crown of thorns from the cross and cover the cross with flowers or paper butterflies. If you wish, place a bowl of Easter eggs at the foot of the cross. Keep the Christ candle and the open Bible.

Weekly Family Worship Ritual for the Resurrection of the Lord
(Choose which time you will celebrate the resurrection of the Lord: Easter Eve,
Easter Day, or Easter Evening. Look in the Activities section for instructions.)

Leader: *Today marks the beginning of the Easter Season, when we celebrate the resurrection of the Lord. We celebrate the mystery of Easter: that Jesus lived, died, and now lives in a new way.*

Reader: Read the story of the resurrection of the Lord according to the Gospel of Matthew 28:1-10. (If your church follows the lectionary readings, use the gospel reading of the resurrection story which will be read in church.)

Leader: *God became human in Jesus. Jesus taught people. Jesus healed people. They questioned, "Who are you?" And Jesus said, "I am the light that lives in the hearts of God's people." Let us enjoy the light of the Christ who lives in our hearts as we continue to wonder.* (Light the Christ candle. Allow for silence before anyone responds to each "I wonder" statement.)

* *I wonder why the guards were afraid.*
* *I wonder why the angel told the women not to be afraid.*
* *I wonder why the angel offered to show the women the place where Jesus lay.*
* *I wonder why the angel told the women to tell the disciples that Jesus had been raised and would go ahead of them to Galilee.*
* *I wonder if you have ever felt both joy and fear at the same time.*
* *I wonder how the women felt when Jesus appeared to them.*
* *I wonder why Jesus said to the women, "Do not be afraid."*
* *I wonder why early Christians as well as contemporary Christians baptize on Easter.*
* *I wonder why we remember our baptism during the Easter Season.*

Prayer: *O God, sometimes just like the women we find ourselves afraid to believe the mystery of Easter: that Jesus died and yet lives. Help us to accept the good news that Jesus lives with us in a new way. Amen.*

Leader: As the assigned person extinguishes the candle, say, *Watch while we change the light of Jesus. Now the light lives in all of God's creation. Now the light lives in our hearts and the hearts of all God's people.*

Weekly Family Worship Ritual for the
Second to the Sixth Sundays of the Easter Season

Leader: *Today marks the* (second, third, and so on) *Sunday of the Easter Season. During the Great Fifty Days of Easter, we continue to celebrate the presence of the risen Christ among us.*

Reader: Each Sunday, read a different gospel story of an appearance of Jesus to the disciples.

Second Sunday: Matthew 28:16-20

Third Sunday: Mark 16:9-13

Fourth Sunday: Mark 16:14-18

Fifth Sunday: Luke 24:13-35

Sixth Sunday: Luke 24:36-49

(If you wish, you can replace one of the above with John 20:19-29 or John 21:1-14.)

Leader: *God became human in Jesus. Jesus taught people. Jesus healed people. They questioned, "Who are you?" And Jesus said, "I am the light that lives in the hearts of God's people." Let us enjoy the light of Christ who lives in our hearts as we continue to wonder.* (Light the Christ candle. Allow for silence before anyone responds to each "I wonder" statement.)

- *I wonder how the persons to whom Jesus appeared felt.*
- *I wonder why they felt this way.*
- *I wonder why Jesus appeared to these people.*
- *I wonder how Jesus' appearance changed these people's lives.*
- *I wonder how you would feel if Jesus appeared to you.*

Prayer: *O God, keep our eyes open and our ears alert to see and hear Jesus in the world around us. May we know the presence of the resurrected Jesus in all that we do. Amen.*

Leader: As the assigned person extinguishes the candle, say, *Watch while we change the light of Jesus. Now the light lives in all of God's creation. Now the light lives in our hearts and the hearts of all God's people.*

Activities

1. (For Easter Eve, Easter Day, Easter Evening) Make an "alleluia" banner to hang in the house. Decorate it with flowers, butterflies, and other symbols of new life. Easter eggs, a symbol of new life, can be decorated with Christian symbols and readied for Easter egg hunts or Easter baskets.

2. (For the Great Fifty Days of Easter) The fifty-day Easter celebration falls in the spring and is an appropriate time to plant bulbs and seeds indoors. Use this experience to prompt discussions concerning how something new and beautiful comes from that which appears to be dead.

3. Choose a day during the season of Easter to celebrate and remember the baptism of each family member. Remember together that in baptism God

claims us as children of God. During the evening tell the story and show the pictures of each person's baptism. Close with a prayer thanking God for the gift of life. Thank God for claiming us as God's children.

Family Reflection on the Season

Toward the end of the Great Fifty Days of Easter, gather the family to discuss how your family celebrations have helped to experience new life. Discuss:

- What would you like to continue next year?
- What would you like to do differently?
- Why is Easter the holiest day of the Christian year?
- How has water shaped our lives?
- How can water bring both death and life?
- How have we experienced death and new life this spring?

Shaped by Fire: Day of Pentecost and Ordinary Time II

The ordinary became the extraordinary in the sanctuary of First United Methodist Church in Seguin, Texas, on the third Sunday of Advent. The children led the worship service and told the Christmas story, "Who Will Show Us the Way to Bethlehem?" As we sang the last chorus of the last hymn, the children's voices suddenly lifted above the voices of the congregation. Frances, the music director, and I glanced around to see what had caused the shift. Our eyes met and then glazed with tears. At that moment we both knew that the children had experienced the movement of the Holy Spirit as they led the congregation in worship. The Spirit of God, not a human voice, whispered to them, "Sing, children, sing!" The children left the service bubbling with excitement.

Frances and I learned later that several children remarked to their parents that leading the worship service on Sunday morning meant more to them than even performing a Christmas program on Sunday evening. Somehow the children understood that the Sunday evening program presented an opportunity for parents to watch their children's performance, while Sunday morning's service meant they led in the worship of God. On Sunday morning they became God's Word. An intentional decision by the staff to provide this opportunity for children made room for the Holy Spirit to work in their lives. Shaped by a moment of fire, the children returned home to the routine of another Sunday afternoon and to another week of school.

THE FIRES OF PENTECOST

Fifty days after the death of Jesus, a violent, rushing wind filled the house where the disciples waited. Tongues of fire appeared, one resting on each disciple. This fire did not consume but indicated the coming of the Holy Spirit into each of the disciples' lives, empowering them to embody the ministry that Jesus had begun. The fire and the winds of the Holy Spirit shaped the birth of the church of Jesus Christ. Peter announced to the Pentecost crowd that the Jesus whom they had crucified, God had raised and made both Lord and Messiah.

Into the ordinary lives of these disciples came that moment of Pentecost when the energizing fire of the Holy Spirit lifted them above their ordinariness. They began to dream dreams and envision ways to live as the body of Christ for all the world. Then the moment of Pentecost ended and, shaped by the Spirit's fire, they once again found themselves traveling the dusty roads of life striving to live in each day that moment of Pentecost.

We remember that your church was born in wind and fire, not to sweep us heavenward like a presumptuous tower, but to guide us down the dusty roads of this world so that we may lift up the downcast, heal the broken, reconcile what is lost, and bring peace amidst unrest.[1]

The Day of Pentecost finds the church gathered in celebration of the gift of the Holy Spirit. Christians refer to this day as the birthday of the church. Shaped by the ordinariness of our lives, we wait for our own moments of Pentecost, those empowering experiences of God's Holy Spirit, to transform us. This fire sent from God emboldens us to live God-shaped lives.

Moses had such a fiery experience. Out in the hilly country, he tended his father-in-law's sheep, day in and day out. One ordinary day—Moses experienced many of these since his escape from the royal courts of the Pharaoh of Egypt—he caught sight of a glimmering, shimmering flame. A bush blazed with fire, yet it did not burn up. Moses, transfixed, suddenly heard God call to him from the bush, telling him to remove his sandals because he stood on holy ground.

> Then the LORD said, "I have observed the misery of my people who are in Egypt; I have heard their cry on account of their taskmasters. Indeed, I know their sufferings, and I have come down to deliver them from the Egyptians, and to bring them up out of that land to a good and broad land, a land flowing with milk and honey. . . . The cry of the Israelites has now come to me; I have also seen how the Egyptians oppress them. So come, I will send you to Pharaoh to bring my people, the Israelites, out of Egypt." (Exodus 3:7-8, 9-10)

Moses, shaped by God's empowering fire, would never be the same. He tried—he argued with God that he lacked the gifts for such a task. After all, he stuttered. God solved that problem by saying that Aaron could go as Moses' spokesman. (The God who can cause a bush to flame and not burn up can assuredly empower God's own people to do the task to which God calls them.) Scared to death and dragging his heels, yet full of God's miracle-working power, Moses returned to the land from which he had fled. He faced a new pharaoh with God's message, "Let my people go." Thus Moses, a mortal man empowered by the fire of God's Spirit, freed the Hebrew people.

Like the children who led worship, like Moses in the hill country, each of us experiences moments when the ordinary becomes extraordinary. We do not choose these moments. We cannot plan for them. We cannot engineer their occurrence. They come from the Spirit at unexpected times and in unexpected ways.

But we all must return to live that empowerment in the ordinariness of our worlds. God does not empower us to live in the continuous presence of Pentecost fire, but to live in ways that will bring God's kingdom on earth.

> We savor the Pentecost moments—the ecstatic experience of being
> released in the dance of the Spirit—but we live in the steady gaze of
> the first disciples, encouraging us to grow slowly, steadily deeper into
> an equally passionate commitment in the Spirit.[2]

As you learn to grow "steadily deeper" in the Spirit, use the inspiration of Moses' and the children's stories to grapple with your own moments when the love of God warmed and touched you in extraordinary ways. Struggle to understand how these moments changed your living in ordinary days. Most of all, remember that in God lives mystery. We can only begin to feel the Potter shaping our lives. We can only know that the Potter touches our lives and changes our shape. We can never fully comprehend the shaping that comes from God.

WHERE THE FLAMES SEND US

Shaped by the red-hot flames of Pentecost, we move to the vibrant green of nature. Green signals that earth, air, water, and sunlight have combined in their ordinary, unremarkable, yet miraculous way to produce growth and foster life in Ordinary Time II.[3] We cannot have one without the other: we live ordinary time open, expectant, and present to the sacred moment, and we return from the sacred moment shaped and empowered by God's fire to live ordinary time in new ways.

Ordinary Time becomes sacred when the ordinary becomes extraordinary, as in the stories we have considered. But Ordinary Time also becomes sacred through ceremony. A ritual can help us touch the holy.

A story I read changed the ordinary moments of my early morning preparations into holy moments. The story told of a woman living in an earth-floor hut in the Outer Hebrides off the west coast of Scotland. She began each day by splashing her face with three palm-fulls of water, invoking the names of the Trinity. Then she stirred the fire banked the night before, remembering that the flame symbolizes the warmth of Christ's love we keep burning in our hearts. I adopted one of her rituals and now, each morning, as the last part of my face-washing routine, I splash three handfuls of cold water on my face and say, "In the name of the Father, the Son, and the Holy Spirit." I begin my morning by remembering who I am and to whom I belong. I begin my day by touching the Creator. Routine becomes ritual. Ordinary becomes extraordinary. Every deed becomes holy.

Interpretation is another tool for changing the ordinary into the extraordinary. When an interpreter helps us to see God in an ordinary event where before we did not see God, it becomes an extraordinary event.

Vallilea, an associate pastor I served with, told me that her father often said, "Valli, the preparation for worship begins Sunday morning with the fight over the bathroom." Valli explained that she grew up with three brothers and, like most families of six, experienced the inevitable fight over the family bathroom: "Who gets to go first?" "How long can he stay in there?" "Did you see how messy he left the bathroom?" Although the fights centering on the bathroom separated brother from brother and brother from sister, Valli's father taught her that worship brought the family back together. In holy space, during holy time, God reconciled them one to another. "When you are all grown up, Valli, remember that preparing for worship begins with the fight over the bathroom!"

Valli's father's interpretation of the bathroom quarrels focused the family on reconciliation that comes through worship. His words turned an ordinary family fight into an extraordinary experience of holiness. When parents merely lament Sunday morning bathroom fights, they miss an opportunity to act as interpreters to help their children see the extraordinary in the ordinary. Depending on a parent's interpretive ability, even something as ordinary as a sibling squabble holds the potential for meeting God.

The Day of Pentecost and Ordinary Time II become challenges for our daily lives. Will this day bring God's heartwarming experience in unexpected ways and unexpected places? Will we experience the empowering breath and flames of God's Spirit to live Ordinary Time as followers of Jesus? Will we use this day to create or practice holy rituals? Will we interpret daily activities and events in our life and the lives of our children as filled with God-given possibilities? Let us see each day in the words of Elizabeth Barrett Browning from her poem "Aurora Leigh":

> Earth's crammed with heaven,
> And every common bush afire with God.

LIVING IN GOD'S TIME:
SHAPED BY THE WIND AND FIRE OF PENTECOST

As we begin to consider the Day of Pentecost and Ordinary Time II in our homes, we have a twofold purpose: to help children to see the times when the ordinary becomes extraordinary, and to use ritual or interpretation to foster the possibility of turning the ordinary into the sacred.

Preparing the Home Worship Area

Change the white cloth of the Easter Season to a red one for the Day of Pentecost, then a green one for Ordinary Time II. Remove the flower or butterfly decorations from the cross; decorate it instead with cellophane flames of red, orange, and yellow, along with a white descending dove. The Christ candle remains in front of the cross and an open Bible in front of the candle. When you enter Ordinary Time II, remove the flames and dove. Encourage family members to add ordinary objects from nature such as rocks and flowers.

Weekly Family Worship Ritual for the Day of Pentecost

Leader: *Today marks the Day of Pentecost, the birthday of the church. We celebrate the coming of the Holy Spirit into each of our lives, empowering and energizing us to embody the ministry of Jesus Christ.*

Reader: Read the story of the Day of Pentecost as found in Acts 2:1-36.

Leader: *God became human in Jesus. Jesus taught people. Jesus healed people. They questioned, "Who are you?" And Jesus said, "I am the light that lives in the hearts of God's people." Let us enjoy the light of the Christ who lives in our hearts as we continue to wonder.* (Light the Christ candle. Allow for silence before anyone responds to each "I wonder" statement.)

• *I wonder why the disciples gathered in the room upstairs in Jerusalem.*

• *I wonder what it feels like to be filled with the Holy Spirit.*

• *I wonder if you have ever been filled with the Holy Spirit.*

• *I wonder why the disciples spoke in other languages.*

• *I wonder why Peter, who denied Jesus, now speaks with such power about Jesus.*

• *I wonder if the Holy Spirit enables you to do things that you otherwise would not be able to do.*

Prayer: *O God, let your winds blow through us and your flames rest upon us so that we may be filled with your Holy Spirit. May your Spirit guide us and enable us to do those things you would have us do. Amen.*

Leader: As the assigned person extinguishes the light, say, *Watch while we change the light of Jesus. Now the light lives in all of God's creation. Now the light lives in our hearts and the hearts of all God's people.*

Weekly Family Worship Ritual for the Weeks of Ordinary Time II

Leader: *Today marks a Sunday of Ordinary Time II. We celebrate how God changes the ordinary into the extraordinary. We look for God in all the ordinariness of our lives.*

Reader: Each Sunday read the appropriate scriptures from this list:[4]

YEAR A	YEAR B	YEAR C

Day of Pentecost

Acts 2:1-21	Acts 2:1-21	Acts 2:1-21
Ps. 104:24-34, 35*b*	Ps. 104:24-34, 35*b*	Ps. 104:24-34, 35*b*
1 Cor. 12:3*b*-13	Rom. 8:22-27	Rom. 8:14-17
John 7:37-39	John 15:26-27; 16:4*b*-15	John 14:8-17 (25-27)

Trinity Sunday (First Sunday after Pentecost)

Gen. 1:1-2:4*a*	Isa. 6:1-8	Prov. 8:1-4, 22-31
Ps. 8	Ps. 29	Ps. 8
2 Cor. 13:11-13	Rom. 8:12-17	Rom. 5:1-5
Matt. 28:16-20	John 3:1-17	John 16:12-15

Sunday between May 29 and June 4 inclusive (if after Trinity Sunday)

Gen. 6:11-22; 7:24; 8:14-19	1 Sam. 3:1-20	1 Kings 18:20-39
Ps. 46	Ps. 139:1-6, 13-18	Ps. 96
Rom. 1:16-17; 3:22*b*-28 (29-31)	2 Cor. 4:5-12	Gal. 1:1-12
Matt. 7:21-29	Mark 2:23-3:6	Luke 7:1-10

Sunday between June 5 and 11 inclusive (if after Trinity Sunday)

Gen. 12:1-9	1 Sam. 8:4-20 (11:14-15)	1 Kings 17:8-24
Ps. 33:1-12	Ps. 138	Ps. 146

YEAR A	YEAR B	YEAR C
Rom. 4:13-25	2 Cor. 4:13-5:1	Gal. 1:11-24
Matt. 9:9-13, 18-26	Mark 3:20-35	Luke 7:11-17

Sunday between June 12 and 18 inclusive (if after Trinity Sunday)

Gen. 18:1-15	1 Sam. 15:34-16:13	1 Kings 21:1-21*a*
Ps. 116:1-2, 12-19	Ps. 20 or Ps. 72	Ps. 5:1-8
Rom. 5:1-8	2 Cor. 5:6-10 (11-13), 14-17	Gal. 2:15-21
Matt. 9:35-10:8 (9-23)	Mark 4:26-34	Luke 7:36-8:3

Sunday between June 19 and 25 inclusive (if after Trinity Sunday)

Gen. 21:8-21	1 Sam. 17:(1*a*, 4-11, 19-23) 32-49	1 Kings 19:1-15*a*
Ps. 86:1-10, 16-17 or Ps. 17	Ps. 9:9-20	Ps. 42
Rom. 6:1*b*-11	2 Cor. 6:1-13	Gal. 3:23-29
Matt. 10:24-39	Mark 4:35-41	Luke 8:26-39

Sunday between June 26 and July 2 inclusive

Gen. 22:1-14	2 Sam. 1:1, 17-27	2 Kings 2:1-2, 6-14
Ps. 13	Ps. 130	Ps. 77:1-2, 11-20
Rom. 6:12-23	2 Cor. 8:7-15	Gal. 5:1, 13-25
Matt. 10:40-42	Mark 5:21-43	Luke 9:51-62

YEAR A	YEAR B	YEAR C

Sunday between July 3 and 9 inclusive

Gen. 24:34-38, 42-49, 58-67	2 Sam. 5:1-5, 9-10	2 Kings 5:1-14
Ps. 45:10-17 or Ps. 72	Ps. 48	Ps. 30
Rom. 7:15-25*a*	2 Cor. 12:2-10	Gal. 6:(1-6) 7-16
Matt. 11:16-19, 25-30	Mark 6:1-13	Luke 10:1-11, 16-20

Sunday between July 10 and 16 inclusive

Gen. 25:19-34	2 Sam. 6:1-5, 12*b*-19	Amos 7:7-17
Ps. 119:105-112 or Ps. 25	Ps. 24	Ps. 82
Rom. 8:1-11	Eph. 1:3-14	Col. 1:1-14
Matt. 13:1-9, 18-23	Mark 6:14-29	Luke 10:25-37

Sunday between July 17 and 23 inclusive

Gen. 28:10-19*a*	2 Sam. 7:1-14*a*	Amos 8:1-12
Ps. 139:1-12, 23-34	Ps. 89:20-37	Ps. 52 or Ps. 82
Rom. 8:12-25	Eph. 2:11-22	Col. 1:15-28
Matt. 13:24-30, 36-43	Mark 6:30-34, 53-56	Luke 10:38-42

Sunday between July 24 and 30 inclusive

Gen. 29:15-28	2 Sam. 11:1-15	Hos. 1:2-10
Ps. 105:1-11, 45*b*	Ps. 14	Ps. 85
Rom. 8:26-39	Eph. 3:14-21	Col. 2:6-15 (16-19)
Matt. 13:31-33, 44-52	John 6:1-21	Luke 11:1-13

YEAR A	YEAR B	YEAR C

Sunday between July 31 and August 6 inclusive

YEAR A	YEAR B	YEAR C
Gen. 32:22-31	2 Sam. 11:26-12:13*a*	Hos. 11:1-11
Ps. 17:1-7, 15	Ps. 51:1-12	Ps. 107:1-9, 43
Rom. 9:1-5	Eph. 4:1-16	Col. 3:1-11
Matt. 14:13-21	John 6:24-35	Luke 12:13-21

Sunday between August 7 and 13 inclusive

YEAR A	YEAR B	YEAR C
Gen. 37:1-4, 12-28	2 Sam. 18:5-9, 15, 31-33	Isa. 1:1, 10-20
Ps. 105:1-6, 16-22, 45*b*	Ps. 130	Ps. 50:1-8, 22-23
Rom. 10:5-15	Eph. 4:25-5:2	Heb. 11:1-3, 8-16
Matt. 14:22-33	John 6:35, 41-51	Luke 12:32-40

Sunday between August 14 and 20 inclusive

YEAR A	YEAR B	YEAR C
Gen. 45:1-15	1 Kings 2:10-12; 3:3-14	Isa. 5:1-7
Ps. 133	Ps. 111	Ps. 80:1-2, 8-19
Rom. 11:1-2*a*, 29-32	Eph. 5:15-20	Heb. 11:29-12:2
Matt. 15:(10-20) 21-28	John 6:51-58	Luke 12:49-56

Sunday between August 21 and 27 inclusive

YEAR A	YEAR B	YEAR C
Exod. 1:8-2:10	1 Kings 8:(1, 6, 10-11) 22-30, 41-43	Jer. 1:4-10
Ps. 124	Ps. 84	Ps. 71:1-6
Rom. 12:1-8	Eph. 6:10-20	Heb. 12:18-29

YEAR A	YEAR B	YEAR C
Matt. 16:13-20	John 6:56-69	Luke 13:10-17

Sunday between August 28 and September 3 inclusive

Exod. 3:1-15	Song of Sol. 2:8-13	Jer. 2:4-13
Ps. 105:1-6, 23-26, 45*c*	Ps. 45:1-2, 6-9 or Ps. 72	Ps. 81:1, 10-16
Rom. 12:9-21	James 1:17-27	Heb. 13:1-8, 15-16
Matt. 16:21-28	Mark 7:1-8, 14-15, 21-23	Luke 14:1, 7-14

Leader: *God became human in Jesus. Jesus taught people. Jesus healed people. They questioned, "Who are you?" And Jesus said, "I am the light that lives in the hearts of God's people."* Let us enjoy the light of Christ who lives in our hearts as we continue to wonder. (Light the Christ candle. Allow for silence before anyone responds to each "I wonder" statement.)

- *I wonder what seems ordinary in the scripture today.*
- *I wonder if something ordinary in today's story becomes extraordinary.*
- *As you reflect over last week, I wonder if you can think of a time when an ordinary moment became extraordinary.*

Prayer: *O God, open our eyes to see your extraordinary work in the ordinariness of our world. Change our ordinary lives to reflect your extraordinary love. Amen.*

Leader: As the assigned person extinguishes the light, say, *Watch while we change the light of Jesus. Now the light lives in all of God's creation. Now the light lives in our hearts and the hearts of all God's people.*

Activities

1. (For the Day of Pentecost) Wear red clothes, eat red foods, make a birthday cake with red icing and a white dove.[5] Read aloud Acts 2, using sounds and actions to bring the Pentecost story to life. In the afternoon, making and flying kites provides an opportunity to talk about the use of the biblical metaphor of wind for the Spirit.

2. (For Ordinary Time II) Make family routines extraordinary or "holy."

Celebrating Birthdays: Take time for each family member to share what he or she likes most about the birthday person. Family members who live at a distance can share in writing. Bless the birthday person by saying, "(Name), we remember the day of your birth and give thanks for your life." As you say the blessing, mark a cross on the person's forehead with water or birthday cake icing. These birthday rituals focus on life as a gift from God and on the inner gifts the birthday person received from God.

Eating together: Community and discipleship grow at the family table. We all need to take time from our busy days to meet Jesus in the breaking of the bread, to feed upon the nourishment of both physical food and the spiritual food we receive from one another in the name of Christ. We need to offer thanks to Jesus for the gift and the many blessings of life. Many families find spiritual nourishment and togetherness as they hold hands around the table while a family member offers the prayer. Share an evening meal together at least once a week, if not each day.

Preparing for sleep: Children need an established bedtime ritual that offers solitude, comfort, and peacefulness. Bedtime then becomes a time of resting in God. Until I left home for college, I followed a bedtime ritual that changed only slightly as I grew older. I always hugged and kissed my parents "good night." My mother sat on my bed to hear my prayers and to talk. There came a time when she quit hearing my prayers, but she still came in to sit on my bed and talk. This ritual marked the completion of homework, the end of an activity-filled day, a gradual winding down, and a readiness for sleep and rest. Spend time together looking for God in the day's events. We can be shaped by the extraordinary in the ordinary of bedtime rituals.

Family Reflection on the Season

Following Pentecost Sunday and Ordinary Time II, discuss the family celebration of the birthday of the church.

- Did this day have more meaning for us as a family than in past years?
- What would you like to continue next year?
- What would you do differently?
- What ordinary events would you like to make extraordinary?

Shaped by a Child: Kingdomtide (Ordinary Time III)

❦

Have you ever stood on holy ground? I have in our church building, but not necessarily in the room you would expect. I wasn't in the sanctuary but in the nursery when a five-year-old placed me on holy ground. That Sunday morning I had acted on a recent decision between the pastor and myself to serve Holy Communion to both the nursery workers and the nursery children. We knew this decision held the potential to shape the children's sense of welcome or unwelcome at Jesus' table. That evening I received confirmation that our decision had been a wise one. When I walked into the nursery, a child of five named Beth broke off her cracker and reached toward my mouth and said, "Eat. Remember Jesus loves you."

Beth served me that evening as I had served her that morning. A holy moment on holy ground was called into being by one of God's smallest ones. An intentional decision by a church staff concerning the shape of God's community at the Communion table in the morning became an unintentional shaping experience for me in the evening. I glimpsed the kingdom of God hidden like a treasure in five-year-old Beth when she offered me an ordinary saltine cracker as a reminder of the extraordinary love Jesus has for me.

Children have taught me much about the kingdom of God as hidden treasure as they come to the table to receive the reminders of God's love. I see God in their eyes and in the look of wonder on their faces. I have heard God's kingdom in the stories from home. Brian broke off part of his doughnut one Saturday morning and offered it to his dad, saying, "Eat. Remember Jesus loves you." A six-year-old born with Down's syndrome broke off pieces of bread each evening at dinner and offered them to each member of his family, saying, "Eat. Remember Jesus loves you." When children make offerings out of the ordinary doughnuts and bread of their world as reminders of God's love, their families glimpse the treasure of God's hidden kingdom.

Jesus teaches us through parables about the kingdom of God when he likens it to yeast in bread which causes the bread to rise (Matt. 13:33). I learned about yeast causing bread to rise with the children in Shirley's kindergarten class. One spring day Shirley invited me to join her class in conversation. I began by saying, "Sometimes I wonder about God. Do you?" I received some nods, so I asked, "What do you wonder?"

One child said, "I wonder how big God is."

Another child said, "God is as big as a giant."

I repeated, "God is as big as a giant."

A third child said, "No, God is bigger than a giant; he's as big as this church."

"So," I said, "God is as big as this church."

A fourth child said, "No, God's bigger because he takes care of the whole world."

As yeast causes bread to rise, so the kingdom of God in these children caused their image of God to grow from child to child.

Jesus teaches us through parables about the kingdom of God when he likens it to a tiny mustard seed which grows into a large shrub (Matt. 13:31-32). Ollie, at age ninety-three, represented to many a mustard seed of faith grown into a large shrub. She signed up for Bible study with her daughter, Mildred, and her granddaughter, Meg. Whenever the group entered into a heated discussion, I turned to Ollie and she set us straight. I soon learned that she found turning the thin pages of her Bible difficult. So she sat beside me and I turned the pages—it was one of the few things she ever allowed me to do for her. Pretty soon I realized she did not need the pages. She could tell us the story we studied without ever referring to her Bible. I wonder how many years I will journey before I can do the same.

During Bible study, someone told Meg that she should write a book entitled *Driving Miss Ollie*. But I would title the book *Ollie's in the Driver's Seat: A Shaping Force to Those Who Know Her*. May we all be as alive in Christ at ninety-three as Ollie. May we all grow just like Ollie in our understanding of the possibilities of the kingdom of God. God's kingdom grows from a tiny mustard seed of faith and action to a sturdy, large plant. May we all, like Ollie, be a shaping force to those who know us.

INHERITING THE KINGDOM OF GOD

During the season of Kingdomtide we earnestly focus on the stories of the only true King, Jesus, so that we might grow in our understanding of God's kingdom. We focus on the children in our lives and children around the world as we seek to know the vision of a just society. We search for the kingdom of God within each of us.

Churches that celebrate the season of Kingdomtide do so as part of
Ordinary Time III. The season usually begins the last Sunday of August and
continues until the first Sunday of Advent. We color Kingdomtide green for
growth. Jesus teaches us through parables the values of God's kingdom. Jesus
reveals through miracles the power of God's kingdom. Jesus demonstrates
through healings the possibilities of God's kingdom. God's kingdom grows
in and through us as we study the stories of these things; as we explore our daily
experiences for their significance and challenge to discipleship[1]; as slowly, in the
ordinariness of our lives, we continue to ask ourselves, "What would Jesus
do?" We focus our eyes and ears on Jesus' parables and Jesus' actions for clues
as to how we might grow into God's kingdom people. We look in the here
and now for glimpses of the kingdom, and work for what the kingdom will
be when it comes in its fullest.

The kingdom of God, our heavenly inheritance, can be likened to our
worldly inheritance. Both come as a gift. Both come to us because our ances-
tors paid the price. Both require that we grow into our understanding of how
to live in the kingdom we inherit.

At our baptism we inherit the kingdom of God. We spend a lifetime,
however, growing into this gift, learning how to live as kingdom people and
understanding the significance of our inheritance.

The kingdom of God will come into its fullness some day. The kingdom
transcends the significance of each of us as we strive to live God's will on
earth.[2] The kingdom of God breaks through as we learn to act like Jesus.

The youth of our church went on a mission trip to Laredo, Texas, to reroof
a home for a family without other resources. They arrived in early July to begin
their project. The first day, they spent long hours under the sweltering Texas sun
as they pulled off the old roof and worked with an architect to fix a problem area.

The end of the day found them exhausted from the work and the heat. Since no rain had fallen for months in Laredo, they left the roof uncovered.

They awoke early the next morning to a drenching Texas storm. The youth raced for the van and headed to the house. They arrived to find the family in the yard waving them away, saying, "Get out of here! These dirt roads flood quickly." So they returned to the church to wait out the thunderstorm.

When it ended, they returned to the home to find all of the family's possessions dripping in the yard. The only items they had kept dry were the tools the youth had brought with them. The mother said, "Thank God it rained. The cattle were so thirsty."

The youth were amazed. This family had warned them to leave the flooding streets while they stayed in the midst of the rushing waters. This family had protected the youth's tools instead of their possessions. This family gave thanks to God for the rain instead of complaining about their wet home and belongings.

The youth now faced reroofing as well as replacing the sheetrock in the rooms of the house that had been damaged by rain. But they worked like they had never before worked. The children in the family worked beside them. The mother cooked lunch for all the workers at the church. One evening they worshiped together at the family's church. Pushing themselves to their limit every day, the youth finished the project! The last photograph taken on the trip shows the youth and the family on the stairway of the house, all smiling broadly.

The youth returned to San Antonio and hosted a church luncheon for members of the congregation who had financially supported the project. They reported through video and storytelling of their experience. One senior said, "I got in touch with my roots. I have so much. They have so little, and yet they were all right with that." For three days, youth from upper middle class America joined hands with Americans who live in poverty. Together they glimpsed the power of living for the kingdom of God. The congregation glimpsed the kingdom of God as they witnessed the stories and videos of the youth.

The kingdom of God reigns when the innocent and the powerful can dance together. The kingdom of God reigns when the greatest of the worldly kingdom kneels down in front of the least of the worldly kingdom. The kingdom of God reigns when those who have the most, those who rank first, and those who always know the right way live in harmony with the least, the last, and the lost.

Perhaps in life we make a circular journey. The gifts of inheritance that we receive at birth or baptism can only truly become ours as we grow in our relationship with God and others.[3] As the children of our lives and the child-like happenings in our world reveal the divine way, we gain understanding of the past so we can become new creatures in Christ for the future.[4] It takes a lifetime to understand what it means to live in the kingdom of God as kingdom people.

LIVING IN GOD'S TIME: SHAPED BY A CHILD

In Kingdomtide, God's people make connections. We live with the question, "What would Jesus do?" as a focus for family living.

Preparing the Home Worship Area

During Kingdomtide, we consider the nature of our inheritance from God and how we will allow it to shape our lives. The green of Ordinary Time III colors Kingdomtide as we strive to grow into God's kingdom people. Keep the green cloth from Ordinary Time II, as well as the cross. Place a crown on the top vertical portion of the cross. A crown of thorns serves as a reminder of Jesus, the servant. The cross and the crown remind us of our calling to live as servants of God too, rather than as royalty expecting others to serve us. Remove the ordinary objects from nature placed at the foot of the cross and replace them with symbols of God's kingdom: a package of yeast, mustard seeds, a picture of children, and a treasure hidden somewhere in the worship area. Consider adding symbols throughout the season as you study the parables and teachings of Jesus.

Weekly Family Worship Ritual for the Weeks of Kingdomtide
(Ordinary Time III)

Leader: *Today marks a Sunday of Kingdomtide. We celebrate the kingdom of God as God gave it to us, the kingdom of God in the here and now, and the kingdom of God that will come some day. We will look for the kingdom of God in the world around us. We will try to live as God's kingdom people.*

Reader: Each Sunday read a parable or a miracle from the list below.

Parables

Canceled debts, Luke 7:41-43

Dishonest manager, Luke 16:1-8

Good Samaritan, Luke 10:30-37

Growing seed, Mark 4:26-29

Hidden treasure and pearl, Matthew 13:44-46

Lost coin, Luke 15:8-10

Lost sheep, Luke 15:3-7

Mustard seed, Matthew 13:31-32

Persistent widow, Luke 18:2-8

Pharisee and the tax collector, Luke 18:10-14

Prodigal son, Luke 15:11-32

Rich fool, Luke 12:16-21

Rich man and Lazarus, Luke 16:19-31

Sower, Matthew 13:1-9, 18-23

Talents, Matthew 25:13-30

Tenants, Matthew 21:33-44

Ten bridesmaids, Matthew 25:1-13

Unforgiving servant, Matthew 18:23-34

Wedding banquet, Matthew 22:2-14

Wise and foolish builders, Matthew 7:24-27

Yeast, Matthew 13:33

Miracles

Roman centurion's servant, Luke 7:1-10

Canaanite woman's daughter, Matthew 15:21-28

Bartimaeus, Mark 10:46-52

Ten men with leprosy, Luke 17:11-19

Man at the pool of Bethesda, John 5:1-9

Feeding of the five thousand, John 6:5-14

Calming of the storm, Matthew 8:23-27

Walking on water, Matthew 14:22-33

The son of the widow at Nain, Luke 7:11-15

Leader: *God became human in Jesus. Jesus taught people. Jesus healed people. They questioned, "Who are you?" And Jesus said, "I am the light that lives in the hearts of God's people." Let us enjoy the light of Christ who lives in our hearts as we continue to wonder.* (Light the Christ candle. Allow for silence before anyone responds to each "I wonder" statement.)

- *I wonder what the kingdom of God looks like in today's scripture.*
- *I wonder why Jesus told this story* (or *Jesus performed this miracle*).
- *I wonder how we would have to change to live as Jesus tells us or shows us.*
- *I wonder when we have seen someone living like this in today's world.*
- *I wonder what we can do this week to participate in the kingdom of God.*

Prayer: *O God, help us to grow in our understanding of your kingdom as we read the parables and miracles of Jesus. Help us to ask, "What would Jesus do?" before we act. May your kingdom come on earth as it is in heaven. Amen.*

Leader: As the assigned person extinguishes the light, say, *Watch while we change the light of Jesus. Now the light lives in all of God's creation. Now the light lives in our hearts and the hearts of all God's people.*

Activities

1. The church celebrates All Saints' Day on November 1. All Saints' Day has been a regular part of the liturgical calendar since the ninth century. On this day the Christian community remembers all the saints of the church: people who listen for what God wants them to do and then do it. They live as God's kingdom people here and now and remind us of the gift of our inheritance. Think about the people you experience as saints in your life. Light an individual candle from the Christ candle and name a person you know who lives as a person of God's kingdom. Give thanks for one of his/her qualities. An example would be: "God, thank you for the life of (name), who always has/had a hug for me."

2. Christ the King Sunday is celebrated the Sunday before the first Sunday of Advent. This day is a reminder that we inherit the kingdom of God at our baptism, but we spend a lifetime growing into it by following Jesus. Read Matthew 25:34-40. Encourage family reflection on living in God's kingdom by considering these ideas together (allow time for silence before anyone responds to each "I wonder" statement):

- I wonder what the kingdom of God is like.
- I wonder what it means to be a servant king instead of a royal king.
- I wonder why God wants us to be servant-kings.
- I wonder why God gave us Jesus.
- I wonder what a peaceful kingdom would look like in our home, our city, our schools, our country.
- I wonder if we can think of a time when we have lived more like Jesus.

A celebration might include a family mission activity to help others in the neighborhood or city.

Family Reflection on the Season

As you complete the season of Kingdomtide, consider how your family celebrations connected the words and witness of Jesus to your words and witness.
- What will you do the same next year?
- What will you do differently?

Living in
God's Time Check

ℑ

*T*ick . . . tick . . . tick. How slowly the hands of the clock move when one is traveling with a four-year-old. I listened as her mom patiently answered, "No, we are not almost there."

"No, we are not more than halfway."

"No, we are not even halfway."

Like four-year-olds, God's children of all ages ask, *Are we there yet? How much farther do we need to go to reach the halfway point? How will we know when we reach the halfway point of our faith journey? How will we know when we arrive?*

Clocks, miles, and daytimers provide just a few of the guides that help us to determine our location as we travel busily in *chronos*. We find it much more difficult to find our location when traveling in God's time. How will we know when we truly live *kairos*? How will we know when we intentionally shape others and ourselves? How will we know when we live as God's kingdom people?

The fact is, no tool has been created that can measure our family travels in God's time. Our journey cannot be logged according to the rules of *chronos*. As well, we cannot determine when a relationship with our spouse, our children, a good friend, or a relative has reached wholeness, health, or near-perfection. Our relationships with God and each other continuously build upon our past learnings and understandings of relationships. In truth, we will never know with certainty if we have arrived. But we can regularly evaluate where we are and keep pressing forward.

The statements below are a guide for a family or personal faith "road check." Add other statements as you wish. You might choose to reflect on your faith journey on Christ the King Sunday, the last Sunday of the liturgical year. If you wish to be more intentional in your family faith shaping, you may choose instead to do quarterly or semiannual checks.

At each evaluation or Road Check, read the statements below and discuss individual or family travels in this area since the last Road Check. Discuss what challenges the family faces in this area. Discuss what actions you might take in response to them.

LIVING IN GOD'S TIME: FAMILY ROAD CHECK

Drawing Closer to God

• How has creating a family worship area helped us grow in relationship to God?

• How has God shaped each of us since the last Road Check? How have we shaped each other?

• What are some times we chose the *kairos* road since the last Road Check? When did we choose the *chronos* road?

• When did we listen to God and take another road home?

• How have we grown in our understanding of Jesus as God's gift?

• What are some times we asked, "What would Jesus do?" before making a decision?

• How has our regular attendance at worship, our study of the scriptures, and prayer together helped us grow in relationship to God? What are some areas where we might improve?

Reaching Out to Our Neighbors

• What are some times we simplified our lifestyle to help others?

• When did we physically work to help others in the community (serving at soup kitchens, building homes, repairing homes, doing yard work for the elderly, participating in a toy drive for needy kids)?

• When did we increase our monetary gifts to the mission work of the church? How did these gifts enhance the family's relationship with God?

• What are some times we spoke out on issues of justice and fairness for others? How did our speaking out shape us individually and as a family?

• When did family members work to bring the kingdom of God on earth? How did these experiences shape us? How they will make a difference in how we live in the future?

Families preparing for the birth of a child or the arrival of an adopted one often spend countless hours reading about the psychological, emotional, physical, and mental development of children. As children grow, parents routinely check developmental charts. They note their children's progress or lack thereof. If you listen to parental conversations, parents seldom describe their children as average. A six-month-old baby may be described as developmentally "advanced" or "delayed." Accordingly, the parents search anxiously for an early childhood school that will meet the needs of their child.

Few parents rush to their pastor or Christian educator in search of charts or books describing spiritual development. Few parents become overly anxious regarding their child's spiritual growth. Few parents describe their child's spiritual growth as advanced, delayed, or average. And yet as Christians we must not forget the importance of inner shaping. God cares about the shape of our hearts. God cares how we unintentionally and intentionally shape those persons and things around us. God cares whether families intentionally seek to live *kairos*, offering their children the gift of a growing relationship with God. Out of great love, God gives us freedom of choice. God calls us to choose love—to love our neighbors as ourselves; to live like Jesus; to train our children by plan and example how to choose the *kairos* road. By these means, God desires that we will draw ever closer to being the kingdom people God created us to be.

Small-group Guidance

Preparing the Worship Area

Set up an Advent wreath with a Christ candle in the center on a blue or purple cloth. Place figures of Mary, Joseph, and baby Jesus in front of the white candle or the wreath. If you wish, place a cross behind the Advent wreath. You'll need a small candlelighter and -snuffer.

Leader: To help us celebrate this mystery of Christmas, we light the candles of those who helped us to wait: the (first purple) candle of the prophets, the (second purple) candle of the Holy Family, the (pink) candle of the shepherds, and the (third purple) candle of the wise men. We light the Christ candle to remember God's gift of Jesus to us. Let us enjoy the light of Christ that lives in our hearts.

Read Matthew 25:1-13 and reflect together:

- I wonder what this scripture tells us about the season of Advent.
- I wonder what it tells us about waiting.
- I wonder what it tells us about preparation.
- I wonder how we keep awake.
- I wonder if you find this passage appropriate for Advent.

Leader: Advent marks the beginning of a new church year, a time of preparing to celebrate the mystery of Christmas, a time of entering the mystery of waiting. Let's talk about how this chapter has shaped our thinking.

- Think of a time we stood at a crossroads. What was it like?
- What faith issues did our crossroads cause us to struggle with?
- What pivotal questions were asked of us?
- How was this a time of waiting in our lives?
- What pivotal waiting times have we experienced?
- How did we spend this waiting time?
- What is *chronos*? What is *kairos*? Which shapes our lives? Would we like to make changes in the kind of time that shapes our lives?

Leader: Let's talk about intentional faith shaping in our families.

- During previous Advent seasons, what family rituals have prepared us to celebrate the mystery of Christmas?
- As a family, how will we wait and prepare during this Advent season? How will we teach our children to wait?
- How will we address the paradoxes of this season? How will we handle the emotions of this season?
- What will we give up from our lives of *chronos* in order to slow down, turn inward, and live *kairos*? Remember to take small steps, or it will become too overwhelming.

Let us share with each other our family plans for intentionally living *kairos* during Advent. Make a covenant to support one another in these plans.

Prayer: Most gracious God, teach us to wait and prepare during this season of Advent. Help us as a family to give up some of our secular activities of *chronos* in order to live moments of *kairos.* May we open our hearts to be shaped in your likeness. Send us forth with the light of Christ in our hearts, so that we might shape others in your likeness. Amen.

Leader: (As you extinguish the purple and pink candles, say,) We extinguish the light of all those gathered at the manger: the light of the prophets, the light of the Holy Family, the light of the shepherds, and the light of the wise men. Watch while we change the light of Jesus. (Extinguish the Christ candle.) Now the light lives in all of God's creation. Now the light lives in our hearts and the hearts of all God's people.

GUIDE FOR ADULT DISCUSSION GROUP: CHRISTMAS SEASON

Preparing the Worship Area

Set up the Advent wreath with the Christ candle in the center of a white cloth on the table. Place the nativity figures inside the wreath. If you wish, place a cross behind the Advent wreath. You'll need a small candlelighter and -snuffer.

Leader: Today we light the Christ candle to remember God's gift to us of Jesus. Let us enjoy the light of Christ that lives in our hearts.

Read John 1:1-5, 14-18 and reflect together:

- I wonder what this scripture tells us about the mystery of Christmas.
- I wonder how the Word became flesh.
- I wonder if Jesus was part of God in the beginning.

• I wonder what the Bible means when it says "the Word was God."
• I wonder how God made all of creation. (Read Genesis 1:1-2:3.)
• I wonder how God made Jesus.

Leader: Christmas celebrates the gift of God's love to us in Jesus. We give gifts of love to family and friends as part of this high holy season.

• Why does the Christmas Season last for more than one day?
• What mystery does God reveal during the Christmas Season?
• What should this mystery say to us about how we celebrate as families?
• What can we give Jesus this Christmas?
• What Christmas or other gifts have we received that reflect the "gift of self"?
• What do we say when someone pays us a compliment? Does our response to a compliment show that we have accepted it as a gift?
• Describe how members of your family open gifts. Consider how family members have received the gift of Jesus. How can we work in our families to explore the relationship between the way we receive any gift and the way we receive God's gift of Jesus?

Leader: Let's talk about intentional faith shaping in our families.

• During previous Christmas Seasons, how has our family celebrated the gift of Jesus?
• Discuss how as a family you will celebrate the gift of Jesus during this season.

• How will we help our children learn to give gifts of self?

• How will we help our children learn to accept gifts in love?

• How will we practice the art of giving and receiving in love throughout the year?

Let us share with each other our family plans for intentionally living *kairos* time during Christmas. Make a covenant to support one another in these plans.

Prayer: Loving God, help us to accept your gift of love. May the light of Jesus shine in our hearts so others will know of your love. May our gifts reflect our love and your love. May we accept all gifts in love. Amen.

Leader: (As you extinguish the candle, say,) Watch while we change the light of Jesus. Now the light lives in all of God's creation. Now the light lives in our hearts and the hearts of all God's people.

GUIDE FOR ADULT DISCUSSION GROUP: EPIPHANY AND THE SEASON AFTER EPIPHANY (ORDINARY TIME I)

Preparing the Worship Area

Set the Christ candle on a green cloth. Place a nativity set nearby. Use a gold crown to encircle the nativity. If you wish, place a cross behind the Christ candle. You'll need a small candlelighter and -snuffer.

Leader: God became human in Jesus. Jesus taught people. Jesus healed people. They questioned, "Who are you?" And Jesus said, "I am the light that lives in the hearts of God's people." Let us enjoy the light of Christ that lives in our hearts. (Light the Christ candle.)

Read Matthew 2:1-12 and reflect together:

• I wonder what this scripture tells us about the season of Epiphany.

• I wonder why the wise men took another route home.

• I wonder if God ever calls us to take another route home.

Leader: During the Epiphany of the Lord and the Season after the Epiphany (Ordinary Time I) we celebrate that the good news of Jesus' birth is made known to the world.

• How do we understand the Season after the Epiphany?

• What do we remember and celebrate?

• What did the wise men make known to the world?

• What difference did their taking another road home make to the world?

• What difference does taking another road home make in our lives?

• When you think of this season, what comes to mind?

• How does Jesus' baptism and our baptism relate to the Season after the Epiphany? Does baptism have anything to say about which road we take home?

• What story follows Jesus' baptism in Matthew? What does God call us, as baptized children, to do?

• If we were to draw life maps, could we identify times (abrupt turns) when perhaps God called us to take another road home? Do we think God calls us to take another road now?

Let us share with each other our family plans for making this season a time of considering what it means to take different and uncharted routes home. Make a covenant to support one another in these plans.

Prayer: Most gracious God, guide us as we plan how to celebrate the Epiphany of the Lord and the Season after the Epiphany in our homes. Help us to take your uncharted routes so that others might know more of Jesus. Amen.

Leader: (As you extinguish the Christ candle, say,) Watch while we change the light of Jesus. Now the light lives in all of God's creation. Now the light lives in our hearts and the hearts of all God's people.

GUIDE FOR ADULT DISCUSSION: LENT

Preparing the Worship Area

Place the cross on a purple cloth. Hang a crown of thorns on the cross. Place the Christ candle in front of the cross. Place an open Bible in front of the Christ candle. You'll need a small candlelighter and -snuffer.

Leader: God became human in Jesus. Jesus taught people. Jesus healed people. They questioned, "Who are you?" And Jesus said, "I am the light that lives in the hearts of God's people." Let us enjoy the light of Christ that lives in our hearts. (Light the Christ candle.)

Read Joel 2:12-18 and/or Matthew 6:1-6 and reflect together:

• I wonder why the Lord says, "Return to me with all your heart," not "Return to me with all your mind."
• I wonder what it means to "rend your heart."
• I wonder why Jesus tells us to fast, pray, and give alms in secret.
• I wonder what praying, giving alms, and fasting in secret has to do with living from the heart.
• I wonder why we mark our foreheads with a cross at the beginning of Lent.

Leader: We focus on the life of Jesus during the season of Lent. We walk with Jesus the way of the cross. We work to live from our hearts what we know with our heads.

- On what do we focus during the season of Lent?
- Why do we consider Lent a season of introspection?
- In the past, have our families considered making difficult decisions a part of faith development? What difference could this make in our families?
- Which of the spiritual movements—fasting, prayer, almsgiving, and making difficult decisions—will our families find most difficult to incorporate into their lives? Which might our families find most meaningful?
- Do children or adults find it easier to live from the heart what they know with their heads? Why?
- What meaning has Lent held for our family in the past?

After reading this chapter, how will our families plan to make Lent more meaningful? Let us share with each other. Make a covenant to support one another in these plans.

Prayer: Most gracious God, help us to keep our eyes upon Jesus during these forty days of Lent. Help us to follow Jesus and learn to live from the heart what we know with our heads. Strengthen us in our commitment to fast, pray, give alms, and make difficult decisions during these forty days. Amen.

Leader: (As you extinguish the Christ candle, say,) Watch while we change the light of Jesus. Now the light lives in all of God's creation. Now the light lives in our hearts and the hearts of all God's people.

GUIDE FOR ADULT DISCUSSION GROUP: EASTER

Preparing the Worship Area

Place a white cloth on a table. Decorate a cross with flowers or butterflies. Place an open Bible at the foot of the cross. Set the Christ candle close by or between the cross and Bible. You'll need a candlelighter and -snuffer.

Leader: God became human in Jesus. Jesus taught people. Jesus healed people. They questioned, "Who are you?" And Jesus said, "I am the light that lives in the hearts of God's people." Let us enjoy the light of Christ that lives in our hearts. (Light the Christ candle.)

Read the Easter story from each of the Gospels: Matthew 28:1-10; Mark 16:1-8; Luke 24:1-12; John 20:1-10. Reflect together:

• I wonder how the Word of the Lord might be understood in these stories.
• I wonder how we would have reacted to the empty tomb.

Leader: Easter marks the Season when we celebrate the resurrection of the Lord. We celebrate the mystery of Easter: that Jesus lived, died, and now lives in a new way.

• What is the theme of the Season of Easter?
• When we think of this Season, what comes to mind?
• How do the death and resurrection of Jesus call us to new life during the Season of Easter?
• Let us identify times of death in our lives. Did we finally experience new life in these times of death?

• Why did the early Christians, and why do some churches today, baptize on Easter Sunday?

Leader: Most families celebrate Easter Sunday, but few celebrate the Season of Easter. We can begin to do this by choosing to intentionally celebrate the Fifty Days of the Season.

• How have our families celebrated Easter Sunday in the past?
• Read the story of Jesus' baptism in Luke 3:21-22. What is baptism? How have the waters of baptism shaped lives?
• What is resurrection living? Talk about "new life" experiences.
• What will we do in our homes to intentionally help family members to see that with every ending comes a beginning? Do family members understand beginnings as experiences of new life? Of resurrection living?
• What questions have our children asked about death? What do we anticipate they may ask about death, in particular Jesus' death, this year? How might we answer their questions about death?

Let us share with each other how we will intentionally celebrate Easter. Make a covenant to support one another in these plans.

Prayer: Most gracious God, we give thanks for the life, death, and resurrection of Jesus. Remind us that all endings have beginnings and all beginnings have endings. In each ending, help us to find new life in Jesus, so that we may live as a resurrected people. Amen.

Leader: (As you extinguish the Christ candle, say,) Watch while we change the light of Jesus. Now the light lives in all of God's creation. Now the light lives in our hearts and the hearts of all God's people.

GUIDE FOR ADULT DISCUSSION GROUP:

DAY OF PENTECOST

(Note: Following are two study sessions for the Day of Pentecost and Ordinary Time II. Your group may prefer to do one long session.)

Preparing the Worship Area

Set the Christ candle on a red cloth in front of the cross. Place a descending dove in the center of the cross. You'll need a candlelighter and -snuffer.

Leader: God became human in Jesus. Jesus taught people. Jesus healed people. They questioned, "Who are you?" And Jesus said, "I am the light that lives in the hearts of God's people." Let us enjoy the light of Christ that lives in our hearts. (Light the Christ candle.)

Divide the group into two small groups. Ask one group to read the story of Moses' call in Exodus 3:1-12; ask the other group to read the Pentecost story in Acts 2:1-21. Read silently or aloud. In each small group, answer these questions:

• I wonder what phrase catches your attention.
• I wonder what role fire or flame played in the story.
• I wonder how your church celebrates the Day of Pentecost. Does your congregation celebrate the Day of Pentecost and then enter Ordinary Time, or follow some other practice?

Leader: Pentecost marks the birth of the church. We celebrate the coming of the Holy Spirit into each of our lives, empowering and energizing us to embody the ministry of Jesus Christ.

• What have been life-changing moments for you?

• A burning bush caught Moses' attention. What caught your attention in your life-changing moment?

• How did you feel? Were you empowered to do something you otherwise might not have been able to do?

Let's discuss how your family has celebrated Pentecost in past years. How would you like to celebrate Pentecost this year? Make a covenant to support one another in these plans.

Prayer: O God, let your winds blow through us and your flames rest upon us so that we may be filled with your Holy Spirit. May your Spirit guide us and enable us to do those things you would have us do. Amen.

Leader: (As you extinguish the Christ candle say,) Watch while we change the light of Jesus. Now the light lives in all of God's creation. Now the light lives in our hearts and the hearts of all God's people.

GUIDE FOR ADULT STUDY SESSION: ORDINARY TIME II

Preparing the Worship Area

Set the Christ candle on a green cloth in front of the cross. Set at the foot of the cross some symbolic reminders of Ordinary Time for your family: birthday candles, report cards, photo albums.

Leader: God became human in Jesus. Jesus taught people. Jesus healed people. They questioned, "Who are you?" And Jesus said, "I am the light that lives in the hearts of God's people. Let us enjoy the light of Christ that lives in our hearts. (Light the Christ candle.)

Read Genesis 25:29-34 and Genesis 27:1-45. Reflect together:

• The story of Jacob and Esau tells of the challenges of ordinary family life. I wonder what seems ordinary in this story.

• A family ritual enters into the intrigue of this story. Discuss the family ritual.

• I wonder if this ritual made holy the passing of God's blessing from generation to generation. Can family rituals originally considered holy become divisive?

• I wonder if divisive family rituals can be redesigned or new rituals developed to bring cohesion to family life.

• I wonder how you can do away with rituals that have outlived their usefulness.

Leader: In Ordinary Time II we are all called to live our extraordinary, "Pentecost" moments throughout our ordinary lives. We look for God in all the moments of our lives.

• As fast as you can, write ten "I am . . ." statements about yourself— whatever comes to mind. Find a partner and share some or all of your statements. Give feedback to each other: in your "I am" statements does it seem that the world defines you, or do your statements reflect the Holy Spirit and the Spirit's gifts in your life? Share your learnings with the group.

• Review the two ways ordinary occurrences become sacred: first, when God makes an unexpected appearance as God did with Moses from the burning bush, and second, when ritual or interpretation turns the ordinary into the extraordinary or sacred. Name a time in your life or in the life of your family when an event occurred like the one Moses experienced. Then consider how you use ceremony or rituals in your family to make the ordinary extraordinary. Think of interpretations you give to ordinary things that keep them ordinary instead of making them sacred. Remember Valli's story. Think of times when through interpretation, you have made the ordinary sacred.

What changes would you like to make in your family to make the ordinary sacred? Let us share our plans to do so. Make a covenant to support one another in these plans.

Prayer: O God, open our eyes to see your extraordinary work in the ordinariness of our world. Change our ordinary lives to reflect your extraordinary love. Amen.

Leader: (As you extinguish the Christ candle, say,) Watch while we change the light of Jesus. Now the light lives in all of God's creation. Now the light lies in our hearts and the hearts of all God's people.

GUIDE FOR ADULT DISCUSSION GROUP:
KINGDOMTIDE (ORDINARY TIME III)

Preparing the Worship Area
Keep the green cloth from the Day of Pentecost and Ordinary Time. Add a crown of thorns to the cross. Place symbols of God's kingdom around the foot of the cross, such as a package of yeast, mustard seeds, a picture of children, and a hidden treasure.

Leader: God became human in Jesus. Jesus taught people. Jesus healed people. They questioned, "Who are you?" And Jesus said, "I am the light that lives in the hearts of God's people." Let us enjoy the light of Christ that lives in our hearts. (Light the Christ candle.)

Read Matthew 3:13-17; 4:12-17; 6:25-34; Isaiah 9:2-7; 11:1-9. Divide the group into small groups of three. Assign one or two of these passages to each small group, then reflect together:

- I wonder what these passages tell us about the kingdom of God.
- I wonder what we remember and celebrate during the season of Kingdomtide.
- I wonder what it means to be a servant-king instead of a royal king.
- I wonder what a peaceful kingdom would look like in our homes, our city, our schools, and our country.

Leader: During Kingdomtide we ask the question, "What would Jesus do?" as we focus on the teachings and healings of Jesus to understand the kingdom of God. We inherit the kingdom of God through our baptism. We strive to grow in our living into the kingdom of God. We await the coming of the kingdom of God.

- How important is it to celebrate Kingdomtide as part of Ordinary Time?
- How do we feel about our earthly inheritance?
- Have we thought much of our kingly inheritance?
- Can we name times when we have glimpsed the kingdom of God?

• Can we think of times when we have experienced the kingdom of God in children?

• Can we see that we have grown into our identity as children of the kingdom of God?

Leader: How have your families celebrated Kingdomtide in past years? How do our churches celebrate Kingdomtide?

• What do our families do to celebrate times of beginnings, especially the beginning of school? How do we as families decide which and how many activities we'll take on during this season? How do we think the words and witness of Jesus transform our words and witness?

• Discuss why children experience the beginning of a new school year and new activities with fear. How can we help our children handle their fears?

• Read Luke 2:41-52 and Matthew 12:46-50. Discuss what these passages have to say about "letting go" of our children. Discuss the "letting go" experiences we have already faced (baptism, first time in the church nursery, first overnight retreat with the youth). Why must parents learn to let go at appropriate times? Can we identify examples of inappropriate "letting go" (letting a child decide which preschool to attend or letting a young child cross busy streets without supervision)? Reflect on what criteria make letting go appropriate or inappropriate.

• Discuss the activities in which families have participated to serve the needy. How has participating in these activities strengthened our understanding of living in God's kingdom?

• Let us list phrases that parents, teachers, or spouses continuously use to describe us. How have these phrases shaped us? Do they help to shape us as a kingdom child or do they hinder us? What phrases do we repeatedly use with our own children? How do these phrases shape our children? How might we shape our children more intentionally as kingdom children? What phrases might we use?

What plans will we make to celebrate the season of Kingdomtide in our families? Let us share with one another. Make a covenant to support one another in these plans.

Prayer: O God, help us to grow in our understanding of your kingdom as we read the parables and miracles of Jesus. Help us to ask, "What would Jesus do?" before we act. May your kingdom come on earth as it is in heaven. Amen.

Leader: (As you extinguish the Christ candle, say,) Watch while we change the light of Jesus. Now the light lives in all of God's creation. Now the light lives in our hearts and the hearts of all God's people.

SEASON	COLORS
Advent	Purple or Blue
Christmas Season	White
Day of Epiphany	White
Season after the Epiphany (Ordinary Time I)	Green
Lent	Purple or Blue
Easter Season	White
Pentecost	Red
Ordinary Time II	Green
Kingdomtide (Ordinary Time III)	Green

WHEN CELEBRATED	WHAT CELEBRATED
Four Sundays before Christmas	Expectant preparation for the coming of Christ
Christmas through January 5	Birth of Jesus Christ, God Incarnate, rejoicing for fulfillment of Advent promises
January 6	Visit of the wise men to the Holy Family
January 7 to Ash Wednesday	Revelation of Christ to the world
Ash Wednesday to Easter— 40 days, 6 Sundays including Palm Sunday	Penitence and preparation for death and resurrection of Christ
Begins Easter, includes 6 Sundays before Pentecost	Joy to the risen Christ, the Resurrection
50 days after Easter	Gift of God the Holy Spirit, furthering the works of God the Son
Begins the day after Pentecost and lasts until Kingdomtide	God can be found working in the ordinariness of our lives
Last Sunday of August through 3rd or 4th Sunday of November	Jesus' teachings concerning the kingdom of God

NOTES

Chapter 1

1. Carlyle Marney, "The Nerve to Submit," quoted in *Weaving the New Creation,* James W. Fowler (San Francisco: HarperSanFrancisco, 1991), 47.

2. Terence E. Fretheim, *Exodus* (Louisville, Ky.: John Knox Press, 1991), 207.

Chapter 6

1. Don Saliers, "Living Baptism," *Weavings: A Journal of the Spiritual Life 2,* no. 2 (March-April 1987): 12.

Chapter 7

1. Garth House, *Litanies for All Occasions* (Valley Forge, Pa.: Judson Press, 1989), 49. Used by permission.

2. Susan A Blain, ed., *Imaging the Word,* vol. 2 (Cleveland, Ohio: United Church Press, 1995), 209.

3. Ibid., 21.

4. *The Revised Common Lectionary* (Nashville, Tenn.: The Consultation on Common Texts, 1992) 233-235. Reprinted with permission.

5. Gertrud Mueller Nelson, *To Dance with God: Family Ritual and Community Celebration* (New York: Paulist Press, 1986), 192.

Chapter 8

1. Kenneth T. Lawrence, ed., *Imaging the Word,* vol. 1 (Cleveland, Ohio: United Church Press, 1994), 21.

2. John A. Sanford, *The Kingdom Within* (San Francisco: Harper & Row, 1987), 174.

3. Judith E. Smith, "This Ground is Holy Ground," *Weavings: A Journal of the Christian Spiritual Life 7,* no. 5 (September-October 1992): 36.

4. Lawrence, ed., *Imaging the Word,* 73.

Children and Prayer: A Shared Pilgrimage
by Betty S. Cloyd
ISBN 0-8358-0803-3

Growing Together in Love: God Known through Family Life
by Anne Broyles
ISBN 0-8358-0687-1

Family the Forming Center: A Vision of the Role of Family in Spiritual Formation
by Marjorie Thompson
ISBN 0-8358-0798-3

My Journal: A Place to Write about God and Me
by Janet R. Knight and Lynn W. Gilliam
ISBN 0-8358-0791-6

Christian Parenting
by Besty Dawn Inskeep Smylie and John Sheridan Smylie
ISBN 0-8358-0642-1

The Gift of a Child
by Marion Stroud
ISBN 0-8358-0753-3

MARGARET MCMILLAN PERSKY has twenty-five years of experience working with all age groups in Christian education. She was educated at Southern Methodist University and the Perkins School of Theology in Dallas, Certification Seminars for Christian Educators. Reverend Persky recently taught a workshop, *Our Lives—Our Stories: Spiritual Formation in the Family*, at the Annual Krost Symposium at Texas Lutheran University, led a family Advent retreat for Southwest Texas Conference United Methodist Women, and held weekly chapel services for preschoolers, which included designing a prayer booklet for children. As a permanent deacon, she currently serves as a consultant in the area of family faith formation.